New Conference Models
for the Information Age

New Conference Models
for the Information Age

Coleman Lee Finkel

American Society of Association Executives
Washington, DC

Information in this book is accurate as of the time of publication and consistent with standards of good practice in the general management community. As research and practice advance, however, standards may change. For this reason, it is recommended that readers evaluate the applicability of any recommendation in light of particular situations and changing standards.

American Society of Association Executives
1575 I Street, NW
Washington, DC 20005
Phone: (202) 626-2723
Fax: (202) 408-9634
E-mail: books@asaenet.org

George Moffat, Publisher
Linda Munday, Director of Book Publishing
Trish Thomas, Book Acquisitions Coordinator
Zachary Dorsey, Production Coordinator

Cover design by Troy Scott Parker, Cimarron Design
Cover photo: San Diego Convention Center by Jonathan Woodward

Originally published as *Powerhouse Conferences: Eliminating Audience Boredom*. © 1991 by the Educational Institute of the American Hotel & Motel Association.

Library of Congress Cataloging-in-Publication Data

Finkel, Coleman Lee.
    [Powerhouse conferences]
    New conference models for the information age / Coleman Lee Finkel.
        p.   cm.
    Rev. ed. of: Powerhouse conferences. © 1991.
    ISBN 0-88034-146-7 (pbk.)
    1. Congresses and conventions—Handbooks, manuals, etc.
2. Meetings—Handbooks, manuals, etc. I. Title.
    AS6.F56   1998
    658.4'56—dc21   98-28396
                                                               CIP

Printed in the United States of America.

This book is available at a special discount when ordered in bulk quantities. For information, contact ASAE Member Services at (202) 371-0940.

A complete catalog of titles is available on the ASAE home page at http://www.asaenet.org.

To the family:
Ronit ben Yosef, Eileen Ershler Finkel, Ruth Finkel Fox,
Raphael ben Yosef, Stanley Morton Finkel,
Andrew Duke Finkel

Contents

Introduction

"Don't blame the audience if they don't come to your meetings." This admonition should be tacked up on your wall as you plan your next conference.

If you organize or sponsor conferences or conventions, take a hard look at what you are offering. If too many former conference attendees confess, "I've stopped going," then you, as a meeting planner, had better change what you have been doing.

It is very easy to become trapped in a cycle of doing what has always been done. You simply change the dates, and copy everything else. It takes no imagination, no analysis of audience needs, no exploration of better techniques. It saves a lot of time, of course, but you will end up with smaller and smaller attendance figures at your conferences.

A great conference doesn't happen by accident. Like any good plan, it requires a sense of direction and reliance on proven guidelines to achieve success. Find out what works and use it, and find out what doesn't work so you can avoid designing it into your plan. Careful crafting, creativity, and attention to detail will pay off in a successful conference that will be far from being ordinary and uninspired—it will be outstanding and memorable.

This book will open your eyes to the dynamics that you can build into your group events. It will explain how you can make your meetings active learning opportunities instead of boring time-wasters. It will provide the tools, ideas, and direction to create an experience that your audience will enjoy and will want to have again.

Unless your audience can go back home satisfied that they learned a lot and can put that knowledge to use, you haven't planned well. Using this book as your guide, you can be confident that you will produce a great event—because these techniques have been tested, and they work.

1 | The Needs, Complaints, and Tasks

Organizations are more concerned than ever before about improving the competence and productivity of their employees at every level. In order to do this, organizations have two requirements: (1) to provide individuals with as much up-to-date and complete knowledge as is pertinent to their work and with which they can take better actions; and (2) to develop the skills—through training programs—required to apply that knowledge.

For the knowledge input factor, the challenge that faces business, industry, and the professions is to determine which learning process will most effectively link the raw material of information to its practical, intelligent application. The conference is one medium—a superior one—which can provide that critical link. It can uniquely communicate information with specificity, relevance, excitement, and clarity.

Even though conferences are so widely used, we have a long way to go to capitalize on their potential. Of all the ways in which people learn, the conference, as currently planned, stands as one of the most abused, misused, and poorly conceived forms of learning that the professions and businesses employ.

To reduce the waste in conferences and maximize their distinctive qualities, attention must be given to ways to improve program learning—the conception, development, organization, and execution of content.

A conference is a process of learning for a group of people. The principal channel of communication is through speakers. There are many types of meetings that use the conference medium. They include programs called by various names: management conference, sales meeting, convention, and "up-date" conference (alternatively labeled clinic, symposium, or seminar). Attendees can number from a few to several thousand. Conferences are used by a variety of organizations: business, government agencies, colleges, social agencies, professional and trade associations, and churches and community groups.

What a Conference Provides

A conference provides an audience with several benefits in a relatively short time by clarifying information and suggesting how to apply it. The conference focuses on a broad number of related subjects and organizes them into a logical, organized program. It capsulizes important changes, trends, practices, and new concepts in a specific field of activity or on a theme of concern to the audience. The conference is a major force for increasing knowledge of attendees in two ways: the stimulation it provides through talks, and the value derived from the mingling of ideas in face-to-face exchanges among attendees. The well-planned conference is conceived, developed, and organized to present a program that challenges the beliefs of attendees, stimulates their thinking, and inspires them to look at their organization's and their own approaches to getting work done.

A conference usually will not provide detailed solutions to specific situations. Rather, it can impart ideas or offer tools with which to analyze problems, provide information to enrich an audience or help it to form a basis on which to make better decisions and provide new ways to find answers to questions.

The incredible growth in complexity and discoveries of the modern world have made conferences necessary. We must develop new conference models, however, for the age of information we now face. Unfortunately, many of our conferences today do not look much different from the school model which communicates through lecture—typically a one-way communication format. If we are to make progress, we must step back and consider this question: *What can we do to create a new set of concepts, techniques, and procedures that will make a conference more meaningful, productive, and satisfying?*

Attendee Reactions to Conferences

The observations outlined in this chapter are supplemented by a survey conducted under my supervision. The survey of 1,000 individuals asked their opinions of the value they received from attending conferences, and what could be done to improve them.

Let us look at the reasons for dissatisfaction with the typical conference today. It is evident, from the survey we conducted, that attendees make serious charges against conference planning. While the survey focused on conferences held by outside sponsors, the same observations are relevant to the internal conferences of organizations.

Although there were many complaints, three areas illustrate the kinds of dissatisfaction attendees identified with programs, speakers, and facilities. Only problems mentioned frequently are presented. I have synthesized several observations into the single statements below, using the exact language of respondents under each category.

What's Wrong with Programs

- "Not enough time for the question period so we can clear up what we don't understand or can challenge what we don't believe. There ought to be a better way to conduct the question period so it's easier to ask questions and get more answers."

- "Not enough audience participation. We have to just sit still too long. There ought to be a way attendees can exchange ideas with each other."

- "The titles of sessions bear little resemblance to what is presented. Titles are so vague or general, you never really know what a session is going to cover. You can't decide on attending a session based on its title."

- "The ceremonial part of the program is overdone. It takes valuable hours from learning time. The formalities showcase people not really important to the audience. How many times do you want to hear somebody say, 'Welcome!' I'd have to include many so-called keynote speakers as not very worthwhile in that they never say anything new."

- "The same subject matter is repeated year after year. Where is the creativity in finding a new focus on subjects?"

- "Find better ways to put together an audience of more homogeneous interests. The talks and the questions that follow are so diverse that the discussion has little relevance for most of the audience. Some method should be found to separate the audience by categories or types of organizations, organization size and level of experience. Then each attendee could select subjects that are of greatest pertinence, shared by others with the same concerns."

- "There seems to be an emphasis on making the conference a booze party. We should use more time for education and professionalism rather than socializing, which is fine if not overdone."

- "The schedule of activities should be created with more thought. For example, a speaker often can't hold a worthwhile discussion before adjournment because not enough time is allocated to the session. It's hard to get from session to session in the time allocated, and yet have time to relax and talk to other participants."

- "It gets tiring listening to speaker after speaker. Can't some way be found to present the knowledge without speech, speech, speech?"

- "Why do we keep putting speakers at a meal? It is difficult to concentrate in the atmosphere of dirty dishes, a full stomach and a smoke-filled room. This is another one of those traditions we keep following without questioning what the audience gets from a luncheon or dinner speaker. Too often conference participants have been led to have one set of expectations while the planners and even the speakers have another."

What's Wrong with Speakers

- "A better way should be found to instruct speakers and have them deliver talks that match what the audience needs to hear."

- "Do something about speakers who give product pitches. They should be controlled so that their talks are objectively professional."

- "Somebody should review visuals used by speakers. Too many aids are impossible to read and really add nothing to their talks."

- "If you have a speaker who talks in a monotone or who reads a speech word-for-word, make sure this speaker does not talk for more than 15 or 20 minutes. When a speaker puts you to sleep, nobody learns anything no matter how smart the speaker is."

- "Speakers are too academic. Get speakers who have been on the firing line and don't just talk theory. We need help in the practical world."

- "Make sure speakers are going to cover the subjects advertised in the schedule. It's a waste of time to sit through a session that is not what you were led to believe it would be."

- "Organizers should do a better job of screening out the rambling speaker and the ones who are poorly prepared. Don't invite poor speakers in the first place or find a better way to extract the information they have."

- "Maybe 10% of the speakers I've heard can hold an audience's attention for the whole session. What can be done with the other 90%—a different format maybe—to let the audience learn something from them?"

What's Wrong with Facilities

- "When will hotels learn that chairs with plastic (hot!) seats are not suitable for meetings? It's hard to concentrate when you're uncomfortable."

- "The dividing walls in hotels are unable to shut out sounds from rooms next door. It's tough to hear and you're distracted from listening under such conditions."

- "Temperature control is not given enough attention by hotels. It's hard to feel comfortable and at ease in a room that is too hot or too cold."

- "The lighting may be great for cocktail parties, but it's too dim and tiring for people trying to see and take notes in meeting rooms."

- "The noise, crowds and flashing lights in an ornate fancy hotel can be wearing on you when you spend 24 hours in that environment. All that glitz takes something out of a serious meeting."

- "It's difficult to find your way to the meeting rooms. Hotels should get a traffic specialist to help place directional signs and room identification signs. Many hotels are rabbit warrens."

- "Food at luncheons often is bad, expensive and served by surly waiters. Hotels ought to be able to do better in planning menus for conferences. Eliminate the lunches with heavy foods that put you to sleep. How can you listen when you are so filled up?"

The Challenges of Conference Planning

Many conferences do not achieve maximum learning effectiveness for the reasons just cited. There are many ways in which adults learn: through reading, on-the-job training, observation, attendance at training and development programs, and listening to others (on TV, at school courses, and at seminars). For years I have heard people criticize the lack of learning from their attendance at conferences. Too many have decided not to attend more conferences because they feel their time is better spent elsewhere. However, in a company conference, individuals have no choice but to attend.

It is not that the conference process itself is fundamentally poor; rather, the fault lies in the way conferences are planned. We simply have not exploited the learning potential possible through a professionally conceived, developed, and organized conference.

Probably 90 percent or more of our conferences are planned by people for whom this is part-time work. This makes it all the more important that the part-time planner be provided with special training to develop the skills required to produce a meaningful conference. It can be done. Otherwise, we shall continue to perpetuate the conference of limited results and wasted participant time.

Too many sponsors do not appreciate the importance, potential, and complexity of a conference as a learning activity. People can become extraordinarily talkative about what was wrong with a conference after it is over. But the heart of the matter is that the difficulties of planning and running conferences are almost universally underestimated, even by executives who are otherwise sophisticated, intelligent, and competent.

Art and Science Involved

There is an art and a science involved in developing and operating a successful conference. It requires an insight into professional and business problems, a craft of translating these into incisive topics, a sense of theater, and the time and skill to devote to the plain hard work of planning, coordinating, and controlling the evolution of the entire program.

The conference provides a unique focus on a vast amount of knowledge and on communicating it in a coherent, condensed, and memorable way. Unlike some other methods of transmitting information, a conference provides an unequaled opportunity for individuals to participate actively: to ask questions, clarify points, contribute, and hear others expand on the information presented by a speaker, and to test the new information with others to see how they can apply it once they return to work.

The Goals of Conference Planning

We do not seem to appreciate how hard it is to achieve the following kinds of goals at a conference:

1. Help a group of individuals to learn, although they may have diverse goals, concerns, needs, interests, and backgrounds.

2. Help each person to feel at home among the mass of faces, and allow each the opportunity to tailor his/her attendance to those discussions that will be of maximum benefit.

3. Develop a meeting design that creates conditions in which participants can learn through greater interaction with other attendees—in both the formal and informal parts of the program.

4. Design a program that is paced to maintain the interest and concentration of the audience, and to provide a sense of fulfillment for everyone by the close of the conference.

In conferences we deal with people who have a variety of psychological needs and mental capabilities. We face the difficult task of blending, for the length of the conference, this mass of people into a cohesive "society." We must manage the programming so that we can reach our ultimate goal: to raise every single attendee to a higher level of learning. To do so, we must treat conference planning from a new perspective and redefine its goals. It is more than a casual exercise.

The Conference Planning Responsibility

Conference planning requires unusual skills and background. The job is intellectually challenging and creatively demanding. The conference should be developed by one person with specialized skills. The conference involves a highly creative process. No symphony, painting, book, ballet, or other creative work can be produced without filtering through the mental processes of one person. And so that same principle applies to the production of a superior conference: specifically, the need exists to have one unusually qualified person assigned to create the entire meeting.

Even though the planning responsibility may be a part-time one, companies or associations must recognize the abilities that are required and the planning process that is necessary to follow. It is not justifiable to excuse a poor conference because the responsible individual is "only" performing the work as a part-time activity. The end result is still a waste of time for attendees (and money for the organization). The part-time planner must exercise even greater effort to learn the concepts and develop the skills to produce a results-oriented conference. It can be done.

The planner must understand how individuals learn in groups. The right person to plan a conference as a part-time position should be selected after a thorough analysis of the individual's talents. By assigning the work to anyone who happens to be available, you ensure a continuance of traditional approaches that are so often wasteful, erratic, and unproductive.

Analyzing Ways to Improve Conferences

Too little research has been done on conferences as a process of learning. Even though the conference is an essential activity for most organizations—either sponsored by the organizations themselves or attended by their personnel—the literature that examines a conference as a major vehicle for learning is virtually nonexistent. On the other hand, we have studied, successfully improved, and written widely with regard to learning concepts, teaching techniques, communication approaches, and meeting designs employed in a training program (another type of meeting, representing a different learning process).

The same attention has not been given to analyzing and testing ways to improve conferences. It may be because the work on a conference looks so easy. There also seems to be a complacency about the conference's inadequacies. Organizations must recognize that their conferences are not as productive as they might believe, despite huge investments in them. Conference costs, reckoned in terms of out-of-pocket expense and time devoted to them by participants and multiplied by the number of conferences held every day in the United States, are staggering. Companies may tend to overlook the huge expense because some of the costs are hidden. Nevertheless, they are real.

If these costs brought a commensurate return, they could be rationalized. But how many conferences are unproductive, boring, or even bewildering to those who attend? Too many lack planning, have no clear purpose, and are diffusely organized. Too much showmanship with too little substance is as bad as the conference with a parade of speakers who deliver interminably dry talks.

Socrates wrote, "The unexamined life is not worth living." I say, "The unexamined conference is not worth holding."

Innovative Approaches to Conferences

There is little innovation in design of conferences today. The most frequently used design is one in which a series of speakers gives talks, followed by a question period. This design ensures passivity on the part of the audience. It results, too, in a repetitiveness that becomes monotonous. Few think of or have experienced alternative approaches in design. But we can design more useful, satisfying, and exciting conferences.

More innovative approaches to conference design should be considered in the areas of staging, presentations, and attendee participation.

Staging. Design a conference in the context of putting on a theatrical performance. Give consideration to such areas as lighting and "dressing up" the meeting room.

Presentations. A few conferences are trying to be pioneers through the use of telecommunications. And it does have some application. An occasional talk, using teleconferences, is a good change of pace. However, there are many other techniques that can be developed to vary presentations.

For example, one or two of the speakers do not have to give formal talks. Rather, develop six questions, with their help, and give these to the chairperson, who in turn will ask them of the speaker. The answers become, in effect, the speaker's talk. Many people are more comfortable and articulate answering questions than standing behind a lectern and delivering a formal speech.

Videotape one or more talks in a studio, under the guidance of a professional director, who will vary the shots of the speaker. Use the videotape as the talk, followed by a question period. Once again, a speaker can be put at ease in this setting, without the fright of having to face a large audience.

Some day, we may find professional actors delivering talks prepared by an authority who will then be available for questions.

Participation. Every talk should have some part of it designed for audience participation. The audience can be broken down into teams of two to ten persons who can review the points covered. They can develop questions to examine or look for ideas to add. They can discuss how to apply the new knowledge.

An audience should not just sit through speeches. One-third to one-half of the time allocated to each speaker should be devoted to audience participation. This interactive learning is the strength of a conference.

The Challenges Facing Conference Planners

As stated previously, untrained people often are given the responsibility to put on a conference. It is not so much that part-time planners create inferior sessions, but that they are untrained for the task. Both companies and non-profit organizations use part-timers to plan conference programs. In the case of a company, the individual assigned the work usually is either an expert in the subject of the conference, the executive whose department is sponsoring the conference, or a person given the job because he or she has the time.

In non-profit organizations, an individual planner may be appointed in a variety of ways. It might be a chairperson representing the chapter in the conference city, or the individual might be a chairperson of the national conference committee appointed to develop next year's meeting.

In any case, the appointee often has not concentrated on this highly specialized and intricate medium of learning. As a result, it is unlikely that a conference will reach the full level of professionalism and effectiveness possible.

A pertinent analogy may help to clarify the inadequacies built into the leadership approach taken in the planning of a conference. If you analyze the responsibilities of the managing editor of a prestigious business magazine (such as *Business Week, Forbes,* or *Fortune*), you would find that publishing a magazine is similar to planning a conference. One medium presents information in a written format, and the other in an oral format. A magazine has departments, and a conference has "tracks." The choice of the magazine's authors is related to the problem of the conference

planner in finding the right speakers. The skill in the editor's selection of articles and headlines is similar to the conference planner's ability to identify appropriate session themes and subjects.

It is unlikely that anyone would question the specialized
training, extensive experience, and professional skills required to
edit any of the magazines cited. Further, it is unlikely that one
would have the temerity to take over the editorship of these
magazines on a part-time basis. Yet we do not hesitate to permit
people lacking the specialized and necessary background to plan
our conferences. It is no wonder that we have not perfected this
significant medium. Until we recognize the scale and complexity
of planning an effective conference, we will not take maximum
advantage of this learning process.

Choosing Effective Speakers

The conference planner is faced with three challenges: (1) to select
only those speakers who have the knowledge that will be most
helpful to the audience; (2) to consider, more importantly, speakers who can effectively communicate that knowledge; and (3) to
create a meeting design that will maximize the flow of information to the audience, deciding how the speakers can best share
wisdom gained from studies and experience. It is essential that
the role of conference speakers be understood in all its dimensions, from identifying speaker names to selection, preparation,
support, direction, and supervision.

Conference planners should remember a survey which is
often referred to by speech counselors: three thousand Americans
were asked what they feared most. The reply—with the highest
number of responses—was speaking before an audience.

The conference is one of the most powerful tools that has
evolved for human interaction between knowledgeable authorities and an audience of information users. However, there is a significant difference between an article that the expert may write
and the talk that the expert may present. The raw material of information may be intended to generate similar stimulation and
uses, but the delivery systems are radically different. We often
have confused the two.

The following is a common occurrence at a scientific or engineering conference. An authority is invited to give a talk at a

meeting. The expert will write a learned paper. It will contain formulae and scholarly concepts and language. The authority will read that paper, seldom looking at the audience. The dry presentation will make it difficult for the audience to concentrate and absorb the continuous flow of complex thoughts. Such complicated information requires careful study and analysis, and is more suitable for the "stop, think, and go" learning appropriate when reading a magazine or book.

The conference as traditionally planned is not the medium for the "average" speaker to transmit complex information, though the conference might be creatively designed to do so with a different session format. Unfortunately, the college model has guided our approach in the use of speakers: in it, the professor delivers a lecture to a group of students who usually have little knowledge about the subject, and so sit passively. A conference audience is composed of mature, practical, and experienced individuals who store varying degrees of knowledge in their memory banks.

The ability of a speaker to communicate information with specificity, clarity, relevance, and excitement is far more important than the speaker's subject expertise. A dull speaker, with the most extensive knowledge of a subject, can put an audience to sleep. The audience would be better off reading the written paper.

To sharpen the contrast, let us assume there is a way to measure subject knowledge and the skill to communicate that knowledge. Two persons are being considered as speakers. One has a 100% knowledge factor but only a 20% communication skill. The other has a 75% knowledge factor and a 75% communication skill. There is no doubt in my mind that I would select the second person as a conference speaker. If a person cannot communicate knowledge effectively, he/she should not be asked to be a conference speaker. It is possible to design a session to tap the brainpower of experts who are not good speakers, but not by casting them in the role of speech maker.

Choosing Session Chairpersons

A session chairperson's responsibility is also misunderstood and underestimated. A properly trained and briefed chairperson can make significant contributions to a session. The individual should control and direct the functioning of the session without dominating the program. The chairperson links the speaker's knowledge with the audience's need to know. The skilled chairperson will direct the session, from introductions through the discussion period, sensing how to adjust the flow of activities to make sure the meeting is interesting and valuable for all attendees.

A speaker may present a good talk, but the session can miss essential elements of greater learning if there is no organized discussion period. The chairperson is critical in making this part of the program effective. A chairperson should do far more than handle only the detailed, administrative work of a session. The skilled chairperson will rephrase questions that are fuzzy, probe deeper when answers are off the mark or unclear, summarize at appropriate times to focus the audience's attention, and add to the speaker's remarks, broadening information even further. If, as suggested earlier, a session is designed so that the speaker's thoughts are communicated through a series of questions rather than a formal speech, the chairperson's participation is vital.

Though these enlarged responsibilities are not typically included in what chairpersons see as their role, the conference planner can encourage and instruct them to perform these important tasks. Ted Koppel, of ABC television network, is a role model of the probing, non-dominating catalyst.

Choosing Meeting Rooms

Meeting rooms are often poorly designed for the function they serve. Rooms used for conferences generally have been designed by individuals unfamiliar with the dynamics of learning in large groups. For more than 20 years, I have heard complaints about facilities from those who hold meetings. Meeting rooms in hotels are designed for purposes other than helping the conference planner, speaker, or audience to communicate and to learn most effectively. Hotels and other conference sites, such as convention halls, must decide on their priorities in room design. If their principal business and priorities are to fulfill conference requirements, their meeting rooms must be designed differently. The facility in which a meeting is held makes a significant contribution to program effectiveness and is an important factor in how individuals "feel" about a conference.

Building on the Conference's Inherent Advantages

There are inherent advantages of a conference that should be weighed in designing a program. The conference planner must create a program that will build on these inherent advantages.

- The physical presence of people is a vital ingredient. Nothing can replace the benefit of making eye contact with other people. There are interchanges possible with an immediacy that cannot be duplicated by written messages, telephones, or televised pictures. Conference leaders can get first-hand feedback on the interest, acceptance, or rejection of material. Corrections can be made at once to meet the needs of attendees. Body language that conveys so much meaning is far easier to detect and interpret when you are in the presence of speakers or participants.

- A variety of sensory techniques can be used to communicate information. Messages are communicated with more lasting impressions when we present information that appeals to our multiple senses: sight, sound, smell, taste, and touch. Conferences can use these sensory influences. Also, we can stage the conference with a variety of audiovisual techniques and theatrics to create greater attention-getting and -holding approaches.

- Environment can be controlled. We can select the environment that will minimize distractions and maximize concentration to the learning task at hand—no jingling telephones, personal interruptions, or committee meetings to attend. We can choose an environment that is remote and relaxing, or one that has extensive recreation and entertainment, depending upon the purposes of the conference. But, above all, we can choose a meeting facility that will optimize the impact of the two-way interchange of information.

- Learning approaches can be varied. The conference can employ every method of learning: reading, small-group discussion, individual work, talks, role-playing, and simulated experience of real-life situations.

- Activities can be varied to give pacing to a program. A conference can be "choreographed." It can schedule learning activities, recreation, social functions, and personal relaxation so that there is a balance among the factors having an impact on the mind and emotions. Thus, attendees are not too tired to pay attention at periods when concentration is required. Program pacing can also provide satisfaction and comfort, leading participants to "feel good" about a conference. The individual should have positive feelings throughout the conference—from opening to closing.

- Interaction among attendees can be achieved. The conference planner can develop a design that creates opportunities for an exchange of thinking between speakers and attendees, as well as among participants themselves. The conference, as a forum for discussion of ideas, provides a unique platform for the introduction of techniques to encourage this interaction, allowing questions to be clarified and application possibilities to be discussed.

Improving the Conference

The irony about conferences is that so many people recognize how bad they can be, but do so little to correct the problems. They resign themselves—though perhaps unconsciously—to their wastefulness, their inefficiency, their boredom. But are bad conferences inevitable? They are only "inevitably" poor when organizations will not face the work and thought required to make them good.

Before significant improvements can be made, sponsors of conferences—whether non-profit groups or companies—must understand these four premises:

1. The conference is a significant process whereby attendees can gain insights and understand how information can be used productively. (Our conferences today are not maximizing their inherent learning potential.)

2. The conference is different from any other learning medium we have devised to communicate information. Its dynamics, objectives, advantages, and limitations must be understood and combined with other processes that broaden the thinking, stimulate the mind, and improve the effectiveness of individuals.

3. There is a systematic procedure to conceive, develop, and organize a conference. These fundamental steps may be overlooked—at the peril of producing a typically flabby meeting. Time, care, and thorough planning must be taken for these tasks, which are spelled out in Chapter 3, "The Conference Building Process."

   An effective conference planner must handle a myriad of details. He or she can acquire the knowledge and skills necessary to meet this challenging and complex responsibility.

4. If a company or association has a significantly large number of conferences of any type, a staff member (or members) of sufficiently high stature should be trained to handle the function. Some organizations may create a department entirely dedicated to the conference planning function. The full-time and sole responsibility of this department is to undertake the total program work of a conference. If, as is true in most cases, the work is considered a part-time position, make sure the position-holder is given proper training.

The job of conference director calls for a person of unusually high caliber. The abilities that the skilled individual brings can be applied to a conference in any field. The conference planner does not have to be an authority on the subject matter. It could even be a handicap if he/she is too knowledgeable. The same principle is employed in the advertising and public relations field. The skills that these professionals have are regularly engaged and used effectively by any kind of organization and for any product or service. They do not pretend to be, nor is it necessary to be, experts in the multiplicity of services and products that their clients represent.

Should a person bring only expertise in a subject field, with little knowledge and skill in the conference process, it is likely that the meeting would never fully satisfy attendees because it would reflect the interests and needs of only the most knowledge-able people.

If a conference planning position is filled by the right profes-sional, the impact of his/her effort will have a ripple effect and far-reaching consequences. It will result not only in a reduction of wasted time at a conference, but in an increase in knowledge and stimulation of thinking for hundreds, perhaps thousands, of per-sons. What a potential gain in human performance for organiza-tions and satisfaction for the individual attendee!

2 How Solid Are Your Assumptions About Conferences?

To paraphrase Mark Twain: "We know so much that isn't so!" It is a sound observation.

Many ideas and practices that are flawed are accepted as valid when conferences are being planned. They go unchallenged by those unskilled in group dynamics, and hence bad practices are perpetuated.

Take This Quiz

Test yourself. Note which of the ten statements that follow are true and which are false:

TRUE   FALSE

1. The use of a committee to determine the subjects and format for a conference is the most effective planning approach to developing a balanced program of subjects.

2. To research the subject matter for a conference, use a questionnaire as a reliable technique for learning the problems of an audience and the subjects that will help them.

3. To develop conference subjects with focus, coherence, and practicality, it is best to find an expert or experts thoroughly steeped in the broad aspects of the topical areas and ask them to conceive the program.

4. Speakers can make the greatest contribution to your program if you allow them to select the focus of a subject. This way, they can

TRUE   FALSE

discuss materials with which they are well-versed and which interest them.

5. A speaker should give the audience a copy of the speech so that each person can follow the ideas more closely, underlining ideas or making notes, thus reinforcing learning by supplementing the oral word with the written.

6. To make a panel discussion effective and to provide the audience with as broad a cross-section of ideas as possible, select panel members with as many different, opposing points of view as possible on a given subject.

7. With 200 or more persons at a conference and the audience size too large to allow audience participation, you must schedule enough speakers to fill the time allotted for the session so that there is no gap in the pacing of the program.

8. The chairperson of a session should be an expert in the subject matter and should be encouraged to make contributions throughout the session.

9. When developing subjects for a program, it is best to cover as many subjects as possible so that every area of concern is treated at the conference.

10. When designing a company meeting (management, sales, manufacturing, etc.) and developing the sessions, there is no need to distinguish needs or problems among audience members since there is homogeneity of interest among those who work in the same department and company.

Check Your Answers

Let us examine each statement for validity.

1. *The use of a committee to determine the subjects and format for a conference is the most effective planning approach to developing a balanced program of subjects.* FALSE

I have never seen a committee work effectively to develop the subjects and program design for a conference, and I do not believe it can. There are inherent limitations due to the way a committee operates and deliberates as well as the requirements of the conference process itself.

The conference process is a highly creative one, as already pointed out. It necessitates blending hundreds of details and ideas into a unified and focused whole. Using a committee to design and develop program subjects presents the following difficulties:

- Committee members represent the more sophisticated and successful individuals in an organization. Thus, their points of view do not reflect the thinking of the bulk of your audience, the ones who need the most help.

- A few strong-minded individuals usually dominate discussions within a committee.

- Expedient decisions are made because of lack of time to think subjects through.

- Delays are encountered in getting work done because committee members have other responsibilities.

- The lack of in-depth knowledge of the field of conference planning will result in a program of routine design and content.

- Programs are defined in general terms. The essential and important job of handling the details is left in the hands of a not-very-powerful subordinate.

The discussions at a program committee meeting can be useful if properly directed. Rather than decide on specific subjects for the conference, committee members should exchange ideas on the problems, trends, and new concepts in their field. Then allow the conference planner to extract the most exciting and pertinent subjects.

2. *To research the subject matter for a conference, use a questionnaire as a reliable technique for learning the problems of an audience and the subjects that will help them.* FALSE

The questionnaire is overrated. It is misleading and unduly depended upon as a source of ideas for a conference. Answers are general and routine, are geared to what people think you want to hear, and are written quickly without much thought. You can generally predict what respondents will say.

Most people are not good at writing down their ideas. They usually will repeat those topics that are in vogue, such as "cost cutting," "profit improvement," "motivating employees," or "meeting sales objectives." The questionnaire plays a role in conference development, but it is not a reliable tool for sensing an audience's needs or developing a program with an exciting new format.

3. *To develop conference subjects with focus, coherence, and practicality, it is best to find an expert or experts thoroughly steeped in the broad aspects of the topical areas and ask them to conceive the program.* FALSE

The expert is too sophisticated, too encrusted with habitual ways of looking at problems, too opinionated. Management, too frequently, will give the complex and difficult job of conference planning and execution to someone with great experience in the subject matter who just happens to be available, or to an already overworked executive. This is a gross underestimation of the professional skills required to develop and organize a superior meeting program.

The conference planning process entails knowing how adults learn in groups, how to extract and mold ideas into a coherent whole, and how to design a format that will permit people to communicate with maximum usefulness. Expert knowledge of subject matter does not guarantee an understanding of any of these far more important areas.

4. *Speakers can make the greatest contribution to your program if you allow them to select the focus of a subject. This way, they can discuss materials with which they are well-versed and which interest them.* FALSE

Speakers should be provided with specific details on the scope, timing, and topics to be covered in their talks. Every talk in a program should fit into an overall design. Within his/her given subject area, the speaker should be given latitude to add to or subtract from your suggestions. Never let a speaker onto a platform without knowing whether his/her speech is focused on subjects that will be of greatest help to your audience. You may lose the audience completely by permitting a speaker to discuss subjects that interest only him/her. Your first responsibility is to the audience and its needs.

5. *A speaker should give the audience a copy of the speech so that each person can follow the ideas more closely, underlining ideas or making notes, thus reinforcing learning by supplementing the oral word with the written.* FALSE

This procedure is a poor teaching technique because the audience will read ahead and stop listening to the speaker. The speaker becomes superfluous. If you want to distribute copies of the talk, do so after the presentation. Or if you want to reinforce learning and reduce the amount of time for note-taking, provide a summary outline for further note-taking. Audience members can take notes more easily, but there is not so much detail that they will ignore the speaker.

6. *To make a panel discussion effective and to provide the audience with as broad a cross-section of ideas as possible, select panel members with as many different, opposing points of view as possible on a given subject.* FALSE

A panel should have no more than four members, and two or three is better. I have seen 8, 10, and 12 on panels, and they are unmanageable. Some people believe, incorrectly, that each additional person with a different point of view, however slight, will add further insights and more balance to a discussion. With this

logic, the number could be infinite. In some cases, the large number of panel members is a factor of political expediency—but it is
not sound group dynamics. Conference planners who do not
want to offend any segment of a group tend to overemphasize the
need to have every shade of opinion represented.

The problems with large panels include:

- Repetitious information. Since each member of the panel
  wants to participate rather than sit mute, he/she generally
  will do so by beating a question to death. The more people on
  a panel, the greater likelihood of multiple versions of the
  same facts.

- Fewer questions which can be discussed. If many panelists
  have the chance to take part in the discussion of a question,
  most will take advantage of it. Consequently, the time taken
  for any one question is longer, but to no great advantage.

- Lack of physical or psychological unity among the panel
  members. If many panelists are seated along a platform,
  those on either end may hear only distant voices making
  occasional comments. A discussion is more exciting when
  each panelist can see the gestures and facial expressions of
  the other panelists.

- More "talk time" than question-answering. Usually, it is a
  good idea for each panelist to make a preliminary statement
  which will establish a point of view and serve as a springboard for questions. With a large number of panelists, the
  length of time allotted for speech-making can be tiring.

- Chairperson's difficulty with control or focus. Any chairperson would have an easier time directing two to four persons
  than a larger group. A chairperson would find it easier to
  ensure a more intensive discussion of a question with just a
  few panelists with whom he/she can probe the facets of a
  question.

The planner should carefully select the two to four panelists
whose varying perspectives represent the more significant points
of view on a subject. In summary, it is neither necessary nor
meaningful to get every shade in the opinion spectrum in order to
have a useful discussion.

7. *With 200 or more persons at a conference and the audience size too large to allow audience participation, you must schedule enough speakers to fill the time allotted for the session so that there is no gap in the pacing of the program.* FALSE

It is poor programming to fill every minute of a conference with talks. The audience can't absorb that much information in one sitting. A program should be interspersed with talks, questions, and group discussions. Even when there are many hundreds in your audience, break up your conference into small groups to permit a change of pace. Talk should not follow talk in an endless stream.

8. *The chairperson of a session should be an expert in the subject matter and should be encouraged to make contributions throughout the session.* FALSE

It is not necessary for a person to be an expert in the subject of a session he/she chairs. True, he/she should have some familiarity with the subject, but it is more important that the chairperson be knowledgeable and skillful in directing and controlling both speaker participation and the discussion with the audience. Chairpersons who are experts tend to dominate discussion, answering all the questions or continually adding to the comments of the speakers.

9. *When developing subjects for a program, it is best to cover as many subjects as possible so that every area of concern is treated at the conference.* FALSE

It is important, early in program conception, to determine the key areas the audience needs to know more about and concentrate on them. Don't weaken the conference by taking up every conceivable topic. If you concentrate on just a few subjects, you can give the audience a much better understanding of the subjects covered. You can also hammer home the important subjects, improving the likelihood that the audience will remember the significant details. Finally, you can spend conference time clarifying points and answering questions, making it more likely that the audience members will become involved in discussion and use the information when they return to their jobs.

10. *When designing a company meeting (management, sales, manufac-turing, etc.) and developing the sessions, there is no need to distin-guish needs or problems among audience members since there is homogeneity of interest among those who work in the same depart-ment and company.* FALSE

Don't treat the audience members as a mass of minds with similar needs, interests, rates of learning, and motivations. They are not. Think about how you can make your program meaning-ful for every individual attending. Weigh differences within your audience such as their responsibilities, experience, and the de-partment they represent.

To the degree possible, group your subjects to allow for the special interests of each major segment of your audience. Even though people work for the same company, there are great differ-ences in what they need to know to make more effective decisions on the job. Account for these differences in your conference de-sign. The homogenized conference represents a deferral to expe-diency on the part of the conference planner.

3 The Conference-Building Process

The flow of work in creating a conference can be outlined in 15 building blocks (Exhibit 3.1). The person calling the conference (the sponsor) is responsible for setting the parameters of the foundation (block 1). The conference planner helps the sponsor define the details of the foundation block and records them. These become a guide for further program development.

The process as outlined is not intended to identify every detail in conference building, but to show, in condensed form, the flow of work and some of its related tasks.

1. Establish Foundation

Objectives • Policies • Dates • Budget
• Location • Audience • Social functions

2. Administration

Facility selection • Facility instruction
• Transportation • Staffing • Room
arrangements • Workbooks, badges • Food &
beverage • Registration

3. Research Subject

Field interviews • Questionnaire • Articles
• Committee

4. Identify Topics

Problems • Trends • Interests • Needs
• Practices

Exhibit 3.1

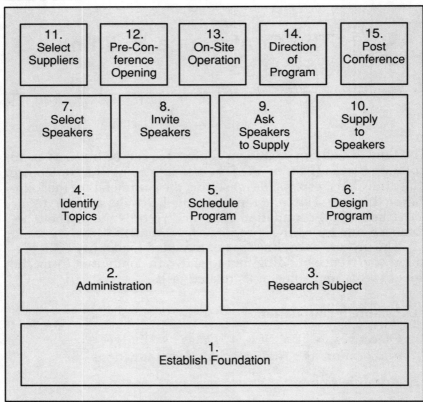

| 11.
Select
Suppliers | 12.
Pre-Con-
ference
Opening | 13.
On-Site
Operation | 14.
Direction
of
Program | 15.
Post
Conference |

| 7.
Select
Speakers | 8.
Invite
Speakers | 9.
Ask
Speakers
to Supply | 10.
Supply
to
Speakers |

| 4.
Identify
Topics | 5.
Schedule
Program | 6.
Design
Program |

| 2.
Administration | 3.
Research Subject |

| 1.
Establish Foundation |

5. Schedule Program

Number of sessions • Timing of day • Tracks • Subjects in each session

6. Design Program

Talks • Workshops • Participative projects • Panels • Demonstrations • Teleconferencing • Video cassettes, movies • Roundtables • Room setups • Staging

7. **Select Speakers**

   Source for names: Committee, Consultants, Vendors, Staff, Editors, Associations

8. **Invite Speakers**

   Telephone • Letters • Instructions • Follow-up

9. **Ask Speakers to Supply**

   Biographies • Manuscript of talks or tapes • Visual needs • Handouts

10. **Supply to Speakers**

    Hotel needs • Travel arrangements • Handout reproduction • Hospitality

11. **Select Suppliers**

    Audiovisual • Computers • Printing, reproduction • Flowers • Photography • Security • Transportation • Shipping • Ground arrangements

12. **Pre-Conference Opening**

    Hotel review • Meeting room setup • Audio setup • Lighting controls • Projection coordination • Registration setup

13. **On-Site Operation**

    Registration • Staff • Hotel coordination • Handouts • Messages • Supplies • Equipment

14. **Direction of Program**

    Speaker briefing • Session checkup • Press room

15. **Post Conference**

    Thank-yous • Bill review • Evaluation • Staff review

Another Perspective

To provide another perspective, the four principal areas of conference planning—**conception, organization, development,** and **execution**—are building blocks that can be put into place as follows:

Program conception

- Research subject (3)
- Identify topics (4)
- Program design (5)
- Program scheduling (6)

Program organization

- Establish foundation (1)
- Administration (2)
- Service to speakers (10)
- Select suppliers (11)

Program development

- Select speakers (7)
- Invite speakers (8)
- Speakers to supply (9)

Program execution

- Pre-conference opening (12)
- On-site operation (13)
- Direction of program (14)
- Post conference (15)

4 | Purposes and Differences

The basic steps in planning all conferences, regardless of purpose, flow from the approaches and sequence of work outlined in the previous chapter. In executing the program, though, you may choose to skip certain steps as irrelevant to your conference. However, still take the time to think through every part of the process. Then your omissions, if any, will result because you made a thoughtful decision. They will not happen simply because you overlooked an activity that might have strengthened your conference.

Keep in mind that this book deals with conferences that last a day or longer, not a luncheon with a speaker, a one-hour presentation to employees, a meeting about a new procedure or organizational change, or any other conference lasting less than three hours. Yet, this material can relate to these other meetings, too.

Take a Different Perspective

Before we review the types of conferences and the varied purposes they serve, it will be valuable to study the makeup of a conference from a different perspective. This involves considering three factors that are psychological and intellectual in nature. They not only can affect participants' learning levels, but, subtly, can create a desirable "pleasure" response in individuals who attend.

The three factors are the following:

1. Mental, intellectual, cognitive factor

2. Stimulation, motivation factor

3. Emotion, pleasure factor

The Mental, Intellectual, Cognitive Factor

How much weight should you give to the learning ingredient of your conference (the mental, intellectual, and cognitive factor) to emphasize content that will broaden the thinking of attendees? This factor has two objectives:

- To provide a range of information focused on the interests, problems, and needs of the audience

- To communicate the meaning of the information and how to apply it on the job

In simplified form, this factor converts information to reach the following educational goal: *Information + Understanding = Knowledge.*

The Stimulation, Motivation Factor

How can you build drama and excitement (the stimulation, motivation factor) into conference sessions? Your aim is to produce sessions that stimulate an audience, motivating attendees to commit themselves wholeheartedly to the material presented, and also making it easier for them to become totally absorbed in the program.

The conference is theater. Consider how to energize the conference. Employ such elements as innovative staging, careful speaker preparation, choice of an attractive conference environment, and special session designs. The conference need not be a grim, academic exercise—and it should not be.

The Emotion, Pleasure Factor

The emotion, pleasure factor—though akin to the stimulation, motivation factor—relates to a different aspect of our feelings. What elements can be incorporated into a conference that will contribute to a sense of well-being for participants, adding to their comfort level? What can make them leave the conference both with a sense of pleasure at the attention paid them and with satisfaction and pride in having attended this conference? These results can be attained by providing courteous and prompt

Exhibit 4.1

Factors	Results
1. Mental, intellectual, cognitive	Learning, knowledge, concentration
2. Stimulation, motivation	Relaxation, comfort, excitement, pride
3. Emotion, pleasure	Fun, enjoyment

service to every attendee, with the cooperation of the conference facility. The emotion, pleasure factor also implies incorporating a variety of activities such as first-class social functions, meals, tournaments, sight-seeing, and recreational and fitness amenities. These latter activities may not be appropriate for some conferences, but they can offer a relaxing change of pace to an educational conference.

Exhibit 4.1 depicts these three factors and the results you can expect to gain from them. A conference should be a blend of all three factors. This blending should be considered in the program planning. The emphasis given each factor will depend on the particular conference and its objectives. For example, you may allocate 90 percent of your conference time to Factor 1 activities and the remaining 10 percent to Factors 2 and 3.

A case in point illustrates the trap that an organization can fall into if it ignores Factors 2 and 3. A conference was held by a prominent consumer goods company. Its products are made primarily for women. The program was to present a "State of the Union" message and to preview the new marketing program. Most of the hundreds of attendees were women. The meeting was held at a posh resort which offered excellent amenities and was located in a warm climate. The president of the company wanted to project an image of a staff that was sophisticated, attractive, and alert. To this end, his pre-conference instruction to the female staff was to dress "to the nines"—with chic clothing, a comely coiffure, and high heels. This dress code was enforced throughout the sessions and the social activities.

Despite the enormous amount of money spent on the conference, attendees had an almost universal negative reaction to it. They felt that management showed a total lack of sensitivity to the feelings and desires of the female staff. They felt that all year long they had had to dress up, taking enormous pride, time, and care in doing so. This conference should have been the women's opportunity to let down their hair and relax and enjoy, in informal clothing, the amenities and environment of the resort. The bad vibes that pervaded the conference and caused attendees to leave on a sour note eventually reached the president. But it was obviously too late to have the staff return to their jobs happy to have attended the conference, motivated, and appreciating the company's efforts to provide a memorable and enjoyable experience.

Conference Sponsors

Conference sponsors can be categorized into three groups, although some of the conferences they sponsor may overlap: associations, not-for-profit organizations, and profit-oriented firms. The programs held by each of these entities and the purposes of the conferences are classified in the following sections.

Associations (Trade and Professional)

Associations typically hold two types of conferences: an annual or biennial convention or a conference with a specific theme.

Annual or Biennial Convention. This type of conference has varied purposes:

- To fulfill the charter provisions of the association

- To provide a gathering place where members can meet informally with colleagues to discuss mutual problems

- To inform an audience of the important developments and trends in the field through talks by knowledgeable speakers and, possibly, a display of exhibits

- To develop a source of income

- To permit association members to enjoy themselves and relax away from work

- To attract and sign up new members through their atten-dance at this social and educational activity

- To gain publicity for the association

- To give members a sense of pride and satisfaction with the association arising from the quality of the entire convention

It will test the creativity and skills of the most experienced professional conference planner to conceive, develop, and organ-ize an educational program that serves the varied needs of the hundreds or thousands of persons who attend. However, regard-less of the attendance size, the conference will never achieve maximum results if it is planned as so many are planned today: either by a national program committee composed of volunteers or a committee made up of individuals from the chapter in the city in which the conference is held. In either case, despite the vol-unteers' knowledge of the subject and their commitment, the pro-gram will inevitably suffer from these built-in handicaps:

- The complexities, the special expertise, and the unique skills required to program a highly productive learning experience are underestimated. It is far less important to know the sub-ject than it is to understand the learning process peculiar to the conference medium. Although sophisticated and well-meaning, volunteers typically do not have those crucial in-sights, nor have they been trained in the conference's unique educational milieu.

- Since the work on the conference is done on a part-time basis, planners must necessarily make hasty, perhaps inappropri-ate decisions to get the work done within the schedule deadlines.

- There is a lack of innovation in developing session designs. The tendency is to follow the conventional patterns already used.

- Less time is spent seeking first-rate, talented speakers. The committees are prone to selecting speakers who are easiest to get: those on previous programs or consultants or suppliers.

- Many of the subjects selected are the more obvious, shop-worn ones.

- The committee is often dominated by two or three dynamic individuals. Their opinions and recommendations often represent the views of the few, more sophisticated and knowledgeable people in the field, not the needs of the less-informed majority of attendees.

- Compromises are made, some decisions are never made, or a few areas relevant to the key steps in the conference process are not even discussed. There is just not enough opportunity to thoroughly discuss all essential areas in the brief time that committees meet. The staff is left to pick up the pieces.

The Themed Conference. This type of conference has varied purposes:

- To present the newest information on a theme of current concern in a concentrated subject format

- To develop additional sources of income

- To get publicity

- To bring in new members

In either of the two conference types—annual convention or themed conference—using volunteers to conceive, organize, develop, and execute stages of the conference will never achieve the impact and effectiveness possible in this superior form of learning. If associations are to realize significant improvement, they must do one of the following:

- Train and develop a high-level, sophisticated, and commanding type of executive and staff who will have total responsibility for all phases of conference planning. The characteristics and skills for this position are outlined in Chapter 6. Since this function probably will be a new one and the department's charter far more extensive than practiced before in the planning of a conference, it will take many months before this person and organization will be able to operate with distinction. Proper training and experience are critical. But, in the long run, the association will benefit greatly.

Some associations now have a position called, in some cases, director of conferences. However, as important as that position is, the director's responsibility is largely an administrative one, performing just one part of the broader work of a true conference planning department.

Under this setup, advisory committees will still play a useful and desirable role. However, they will not make decisions; instead, they will serve as advisors and generators of information for the in-house professionals.

- Associations, particularly smaller ones, can use outside consultants. There are many available, skilled in various aspects of conference planning. The cost they represent will be paid back in terms of the high-quality work they will provide.

  For example, several years ago, Jim Rice, the former vice president and general manager of the 500-person staff of the American Management Association, joined me in a consulting partnership. We specialized in all the steps involved in conference planning, including subject and speaker selection and preparation. We were engaged by companies and associations in every kind of field. The knowledge and skills we brought to each assignment were equally applicable to any subject in any field—just as an advertising agency or public relations firm can apply its expertise to any product or organization.

Not-for-Profit Organizations

Not-for-profit organizations, such as hospitals, governments, social agencies, universities, and foundations, generally sponsor internal conference programs and special-theme conferences.

Internal Programs. These conferences have varied purposes:

- To exchange ideas on ways to improve service and operations

- To announce changes in procedures, organization, and plans

- To review the organization's programs and progress to date and present plans for the future

Conferences with Special Themes. These conferences are held for both external and internal professionals and have this purpose:

- To focus talks by knowledgeable speakers on a subject area of current and pertinent interest to the professionals in a particular discipline

Universities may direct a conference for businesses and may do so to make a profit. But for the most part, universities sponsor conferences primarily for educational reasons, not for profit. Though some of the larger hospitals sponsor many conferences because their field is so dynamic, they do not do so primarily for profit.

Larger organizations—such as government, foundations, universities, and large hospitals—may find it economical and desirable to train and develop a full-time, high-level planner and department, depending on the number of conferences held each year. With the right experienced professional in this special educational format, these entities will find a marked positive change in the quality and productivity of their conferences.

Smaller organizations may not find it economically feasible to hire a full-time professional planner, and instead may rely on a part-time staff member. A part-time planner who has not had extensive training may find it difficult to plan a highly productive and exciting program without consulting an outside expert.

Smaller groups could form a consortium of entities in a related field, such as hospitals or foundations. The consortium could hire a competent conference planning professional. This individual would do the complete job of conference planning for each organization, and would report to each organization on his/her progress. The planner's salary and expenses would be paid on a pro rata basis according to the use that each entity makes of the planner's services.

Profit-Oriented Firms

Profit-oriented firms (companies, consultants, service firms) have varied conference purposes:

- To review programs, progress, and make plans for the future

- To focus on a specific theme of current interest and concern, bringing staff up-to-date on the newest developments

- To announce procedural and organizational changes

- To provide a work/play meeting where executives can relax and learn at the same time

- To motivate staff or customers to perform at high levels by offering the chance to attend a pleasure-oriented gathering of winners

- To give staff a sense of pride in being part of a caring, dynamic organization

- To make a profit on a conference

- To get publicity for the work being done by an organization

Profit-oriented firms typically hold management review meetings, update conferences, incentive/reward programs, and sales meetings.

Management Review Meeting. Key executives are brought together for a review of progress to date, plans for the future, and announcements of any changes. The speakers typically come from within the company. Outside speakers are employed for a change of pace and to introduce other points of view. Time for relaxation and pleasure is scheduled to provide an enjoyable experience as well as an educational dimension.

Update Conference. This meeting focuses its theme on a specific, narrow area of current interest and concern to an organization.

Individuals within the firm are brought together to be updated on developments affecting their work.

A consulting group or service organization, such as an accounting firm, may hold an open conference for clients and other interested parties. Their motives may vary. They may want to provide a service to clients or use this forum as a way to obtain new clients. In some cases, they may want to earn a profit. In any case, the program should be planned as professionally as possible.

Incentive/Reward Program. These programs are developed for both employees and customers. Those invited to attend these programs have attained some high level of performance and have been declared winners in an earlier contest. The winners know in advance what the rewards will be. They usually are trips to places that are exciting and fun. The program for the several days' worth of trips includes sightseeing, lavish meals, and entertainment. Any educational sessions are minimal. New product lines might be revealed.

More attention should be given, however short the incentive/reward program, to producing sessions that are more learning-oriented than mundane. Since the best producers—the winners, or those most eager to learn—are attending, give them something of value to use back on the job.

The multi-day incentive meeting, not really a conference, is typically handled superbly—perhaps because it is generally organized by outside experts who specialize in performing the complete job, including promotions, site selection, sightseeing arrangements, creating social occasions, and arranging transportation.

Sales Meetings. In this conference, the sales force is brought together to hear the results of past performance and to learn about the new marketing program. It is often held at resorts. The conference is part reward and part educational in nature. Since the salespeople are spread throughout the country, often acting on their own, the conference gives them an opportunity to reconnect with the company and other members of the sales staff as well as with management. In addition to the sessions with speakers, time is scheduled for social affairs, sports tournaments, and relaxation.

Although the information communicated in the conference is important for the sales force to absorb, it is also necessary that the conference motivate the attendees to apply their learning to their jobs throughout the year.

Of all company conferences, the sales meeting employs a number of techniques to generate excitement: music, multimedia presentations, decorations, special lighting, and dramatically presented information. This type of conference really does capture the idea of a conference as theater. One reason it creates such electricity is the engagement of outside "show producers." Their unique expertise helps the staff plan and stage the entire program. Other conferences would do well to consider the use of these specialized consultants to bring more life to their programs.

One caution: theatrical elements in a sales meeting can be so powerful and dramatic that they overwhelm the program. It may become, as Shakespeare wrote, "an act full of sound and fury signifying nothing." The message must be worthy of the dramatics.

The Professional Conference Planning Department

Larger companies would find it easiest to develop expertise in conference planning. There is a precedent in their commitment to and the establishment of a human resources department, which improves the competence and productivity of personnel through its skill development programs. The same kinds of results could be achieved in the unique but critical learning medium known as the conference. Management must recognize the conference's potential for producing knowledgeable staff. Then, management must establish a professional conference planning department. Because every organization is increasingly inundated with information, the professionally planned conference can be one of the key vehicles through which to impart this mass of meaningful information.

Build on Trainers' Skills

Consider the kind of person who might give impetus to a conference planning department. Generally, companies already have training and development departments that could serve as an excellent base for staffing the conference planning function. Trainers are highly skilled at identifying needs, converting those needs into subject areas, creating innovative and participative meeting designs, and presenting information in ways which will hold the attention of participants. Building on these skills, companies could provide further training on the competencies required for this separate but related kind of information communication. Some organizations already employ a meeting planner. This individual plays an administrative role, limited to making detailed conference arrangements, which is but one portion of the total charge of a conference planning department.

If organizations are willing to give support and attention to the establishment, training, and development of a top-drawer conference planning professional—viewing his/her function as described—they will be rewarded with conferences that not only improve individual knowledge but also generate valuable employee contribution to company programs, decisions, and productivity.

5 Tradition Is a Trap

If, at the next conference, you continue doing what you have done at the past half-dozen, can you go wrong? This is the safe approach to conference planning. However, such habit is a trap that perpetuates poor conferences. Sometimes it takes an outsider to point out the sorry state of conferences in America.

Some time ago, I received a call at The National Conference Center. It was from a man who said he had been doing research on conferences and conventions. He wanted to interview me as his last piece of research. He said that he had been engaged by a Hollywood producer who wanted to develop a movie with a convention as a theme. The producer felt the subject would have great appeal for a large audience. The caller said his investigations would ultimately be written into a book. Because the caller's previous books had been best-sellers, the producer thought that a best-seller about conferences would provide an excellent built-in vehicle for the movie.

When the caller identified himself by name, it was vaguely familiar, but I could not place it precisely. He was Fletcher Knebel, author of *Seven Days in May, Vanished,* and *A Night at Camp David.* Not only were these best-sellers, but they were turned into successful films.

When we met, we had a long discussion about meetings. He told me about his research, which had extended to two months and had taken him to every type of program throughout the country. At the end of the interview, I said, "Fletcher, you are not a businessman. You're a journalist. So you have an objectivity and a skill at getting beneath the superficialities of situations. Tell me your impressions of the meetings you attended."

His response, though not too surprising, was disturbing. He said, "Coleman, I was amazed at how little I thought was accomplished at these meetings. People slept. They talked. Speakers droned on. Attendees moved in and out of the room. Although I've not had much exposure to this kind of activity, I was shocked at the general waste I saw in them."

There were probably programs he sat in on that did not fit his overall observations. I do not know which meetings he attended, nor their purposes. Yet I was taken aback by his overall impressions. They should give us pause to ponder about how well we are achieving our objectives for our conferences.

"Laws" of Traditional Conference Planning

If you subscribe to traditional conference planning, you should recognize *Finkel's Ten "Laws" of Traditional Conference Planning:*

1. When the topics of a conference are selected by the most knowledgeable people on the subject, 10% of an audience will enjoy a valuable and stimulating experience. *(Of course, there will be 90% who will shrivel up in ennui—if they have the good manners not to leave the room.)*

2. If your last four conferences have been designed with a panel of four speakers in each session, your next conference will be designed with a panel of four speakers in each session. *(Can you go wrong if you give attendees what they have always had?)*

3. There is an inverse relationship between the length of a talk by the average speaker, and the time it takes for a typical member of the audience to think of his/her family. *(Some speakers will have you thinking of your family, where to go for dinner, or which flight to take home, within minutes.)*

4. The number of times each of the dignitaries who take part in the opening of a conference says, 'Welcome!' has no relationship to the depth of warmth that is generated within the audience. *(A corollary law might be that the more times you hear "Welcome!" the less welcome you really feel.)*

5. The more prominent the names of the speakers on the program, the more prominent the names of the speakers listed on the program will be. *(In other words, too often well-known*

people are hired to speak just to attract a large audience—not because they'll contribute material of any substance or value.)

6. When the executive who is calling the meeting believes strongly that an idea should be included in the program—no matter how irrelevant, absurd, or incongruous—it should be considered one of the master strokes of the conference. *(Conference designers who have to deal with this "law" must develop a high level of diplomacy to avoid the penalties.)*

7. Throughout the days of a conference, as the key executive who is responsible for the meeting moves among the members of the audience to get their reactions, it is difficult not to be impressed with how employees unanimously tell the boss that he/she has masterminded the best meeting the organization has ever had.

8. At the end of a talk, when the audience is asked for questions, and there are none, you might wrongly conclude that the presentation was so thorough, every issue was covered.

9. When a fashion show is planned as part of the spouses' separate program, the creativity of the programming for the conference has risen to its highest level.

10. When the overhead lights are dimmed as the speaker begins a slide presentation, and the lectern light goes out so the speaker cannot see a note, a lighted match is better than a curse at the darkness.

Tradition Dies Hard

Tradition dies hard in conference planning. Most of today's conference planners have never attended a well-designed conference. They tend to duplicate the poor conferences they have already attended. This is so with the final decision-makers, the bosses who create mandates for meetings based on their exposure to conferences of dubious quality.

Traditional programming should be regarded as suspect. If a committee proposes a conference plan, be especially wary, because the possibility that any of the committee members ever attended a well-designed conference—much less planned one—is remote.

The reason that traditional conferences no longer are effective is that the challenges today—the flood of information and the need to deal with it intelligently—require new techniques of learning.

The problem is expressed by Richard Saul Wurman in his excellent book, *Information Anxiety:* "Everyday we're bombarded with more data than we can absorb or understand," he says. "To function in society, we are forced to assimilate a body of knowledge expanding by the minute. The future doesn't just hang out there. What we need to do is to gain as much understanding as we can so that, in weighing conditions, we can prevent ourselves from falling into errors. We should understand the broad context of social and economic change that will impact our decisions. There is so much to know. How can we focus on what is important to our needs?"

Four Types of Meetings

The conference is a major tool with which we can deal with the information explosion emphasized by Mr. Wurman—and focus on our need to know. To place the conference in a context with other types of programs, we can classify meetings into four categories: discussion, training and development, problem solving meetings, and the conference.

Discussion Meeting

The first category is the short discussion meeting. This meeting often is called on the spur of the moment. It may last 15 minutes to an hour or more. It is typically attended by three to six persons. Often it is held in someone's office rather than in a conference room. The purposes are to discuss a problem, to plan a course of action, to announce an organizational or procedural change, or to elicit points of view on an issue. This is the meeting that occupies so much time in business and is the source of one of the most common laments in U.S. industry: "I've just wasted another hour of my life in a meeting!"

Training and Development

The second type of meeting is held for training and development. The program for this meeting is carefully planned in advance by professionals skilled in the processes of learning in a training format. In terms of preparation and operation, this program is the most effective of all meeting types as it is practiced today. The program can cover vocational, technical, or managerial subjects. Between 10 and 30 people attend a training class. A meeting can last from one hour to one week or more. In addition to the presentations on procedures, concepts, principles, and practices, most of the time is spent applying knowledge learned in practical situations, with an end goal being to improve skills in the application of knowledge.

Problem-Solving Meeting

A third kind of meeting is the problem-solving, decision-making, or review meeting. This meeting is somewhat like the short discussion meeting. However, it is more structured. An agenda is prepared in advance, and the attendees are informed before the meeting of its time, place, and purpose. The 10 to 25 participants generally are in managerial positions. The program may last one day to one week. The value of the meeting comes from the contributions of attendees elicited and blended by the chairperson. The agenda can deal with a discussion in such areas as a review of past results, formulation of a plan of action, a decision on certain issues, a resolution on how to handle a problem(s), assignment of responsibility to follow up certain issues, or an announcement of organizational or procedural changes.

The Conference

The fourth meeting type, and the one with which this book deals primarily, is characterized by the use of speakers. While other types of meetings may have speakers, the conference is entirely dependent upon them to serve its function.

The conference planner's major functions include determining how to select, inform, coach, direct, handle, and reward speakers. Tradition applied here, as in other facets of planning, may not be in the best interests of a conference.

6 | Who Should Plan a Conference?

Conferences often are planned by those who have no notion of what is good or bad, what works or does not work, what objectives to set, nor even an understanding that specific goals should be part of the planning process.

Amateurs are handed the responsibility for conferences in many organizations and the dynamics of the conference go to waste. Simply bringing people together does not a conference make.

The person who directs conferences for any organization should have special skills and experience. The job description for an association's director of conferences would follow along these lines (these duties can be adjusted for each company).

Job Description for Director of Conferences

Objective of the job—To develop conference programs that are exciting, audience-focused, and substantial, resulting in attendees who leave the sessions feeling that they have benefited and learned through their participation.

Relationship with the exposition staff (if the conference is held in conjunction with an exposition)—To work closely with the exposition staff so that conference topics can be targeted to optimize the number and types of those decision-making attendees who are the best prospects for exhibitors.

Management duties—(1) Organize the conference department, defining functions, responsibilities, and interrelationships to ensure the best use of the staff; (2) Prepare a budget for the operation of the department; (3) Submit an income and expense budget for each conference; (4) Develop a reporting system to inform management of key information on the conference operation; (5) Set standards of performance for staff work on all conferences; (6) Specify the responsibilities and coordination required to best organize the division of work between the staff and any external expert engaged as a resource in the development of a conference program; (7) Maintain effectiveness of the conference staff through continuous personnel training; (8) Develop procedures that will keep control of the work to be accomplished on all conference operation activities.

Conference planning duties—(1) Introduce innovative approaches in the design of conference sessions to make them more exciting and stimulating for an audience; (2) Review all conference functions during the meeting itself to improve their usefulness and cost-effectiveness; (3) Introduce new promotional ideas to attract more attendees; (4) Suggest ways to improve the impact of direct mail, promotions, advertising, and publicity for the conference or the exhibit; (5) Use a wide range of resources to gather information on the trends, problems, practices, and interests of the targeted conference audience so that topics selected will attract the largest audience; (6) Study and identify the profiles of the various targeted audiences and relate them to the individuals whom exhibitors most want to attract; (7) Create a compelling conference program that will motivate the greatest number of people to register; (8) Set the pricing for conference sessions; (9) Write copy for the conference program; (10) Decide on a time schedule and number of sessions that will provide a range of interest for the maximum number of prospects; (11) Develop materials to send to speakers to fully apprise them of their responsibilities and the contribution they are expected to make.

Communication and coordination—(1) Set up communication and coordination procedures within the conference department to ensure a smooth and interrelated execution and cooperative effort among the entire conference staff; (2) Build a harmonious relationship with any outside organization that can be helpful in securing speakers; (3) Work closely with the exhibit staff members to ensure each one is aware of the work of the conference department and that the conference staff is aware of the exhibit staff's work.

In summary—Take responsibility for the conception, development, and organization of every conference to ensure the quality, appeal, and value of the program for its targeted audience.

Although the conference is, of itself, a profit center as well as an educational vehicle, it is important to emphasize that the role of the conference for an association is primarily to attract the greatest number of decision-makers who will be exposed to the exhibitors and the exposition, the reason for being of the entire event.

Knowledge and Skills Required

Any applicant for the position of conference director should possess the following attributes, knowledge, and skills.

Research and analytic talent—The conference planner must gather information with objectivity and intelligence. With an inquiring mind, the planner must probe beyond the usual superficial subject inputs. The information gathered must be analyzed with skill and insight in order to identify subjects of key relevance to the audience. The range of the planner's skill must include an ability to mold ideas into tangible, organized conference form, and to conceptualize a program that meets the needs and interests of the audience.

Communication skills—The conference planner should be sophisticated in communication, education, and training. He/she should understand the learning process and know how to apply advances in group dynamics and training techniques. With this knowledge, the planner can more effectively design programs that will result in maximum audience impact and value. The planner should be articulate.

Imagination and creativity—The planner needs to be innovative, to design a format that results in a fresh subject focus, an exciting program, and active audience participation. The planner must look beyond the traditional approach of scheduling speaker after speaker and must improvise other ways to communicate information.

Broad business interest and intelligence—The planner should be well-read and have above-average intelligence. He/she must keep abreast of social, political, economic, business, and technological developments that may have an impact on business.

Excellent organizational skills—The conference planner must be a disciplined thinker and organizer, able to plan and administer innumerable details involved in a conference. These "details" must be attended to on time and within budget.

Cool head under pressure—Emergencies invariably arise both before and during a conference. The planner should have the emotional maturity and sound judgment to handle these pressures.

Sensitivity to interactions—The planner will be cooperating with many people to get work done, including speakers, committees, and suppliers. The planner must be skilled at working through individuals, getting them to do work, often on a volunteer basis. This skill also is important in dealing with the staff within the conference department.

Independent thinking—Often the planner will work with people who have strong views about how to make a conference a success. If such a point of view is contrary to what the planner believes will work, the planner must be able to express opinions independently and diplomatically, but firmly.

Knowledge about suppliers—The planner should know how to negotiate with and use the best range of support services, including hotels, audiovisual suppliers, transportation companies, and convention bureaus.

Journalistic sensitivities—The planner should have a "nose for news." It is important to provide an interesting story with a special slant that will excite members of the audience and make them want to hear it.

Entrepreneurial skills—The planner should be a self-starter who has a talent for budgeting and controlling expenses. Moreover, he/she should have that rare gift of taking an untried conference subject and transforming it into a financially successful enterprise.

7 | Research for Subjects

The challenge for the meeting planner is greater today than ever before because learning is more important in industry and the professions. In an issue of *Fortune* magazine, an article entitled "New Ideas for the '90s" reported: "The most successful corporation of the 1990s will be something called a learning organization. The leader will ensure that everyone has the resources and power to make swift day-to-day decisions. The leader will have to be the best learner of them all."

In the same issue, *Fortune* quoted Peter Drucker, who said, "As knowledge becomes the central resource, continuing education of already highly schooled people becomes more and more important. This means that the business enterprise is increasingly going to be an educational institution." With this expectation, the conference planner has a clear mandate to develop an educationally rewarding experience. This means that research for the best subjects to cover takes top priority.

Seek Multiple Sources

In the initial stages of gathering information on the subjects for your program, try to get as varied a perspective on ideas as you can. Seek multiple sources of contributions. Never build the conference program by simply sitting in your office and, from your knowledge of the subject, however vast, deciding on what should be covered. This ivory tower approach causes many conferences to miss the mark in terms of responding to the needs, problems, and interests of the audience. You have to get close to those who will make up your audience if you want to have an impact.

In your research, always include interviews in the field. It is refreshing to go to the sources and learn firsthand the concerns of those who are typical of the people who will attend the conference.

I did some research while planning a sales meeting for a consumer goods company. I interviewed a sampling of individuals who would be at the conference. They were surprised by my presence and questions. They had never, for any previous sales meeting, been asked for their opinions. The general drift of comments I received was, "My gosh, management is finally getting around to finding out what it is we want to know. It's about time!"

Whether the conference is for a company or an association, likely sources of raw material from which to select subjects include the following:

1. Interviews of a cross-section of those who will attend the conference.

2. Interviews of a variety of "in-house" people—the person who calls the meeting and other key individuals.

3. Editors of publications, such as newsletters, magazines, and newspapers. In general, these are not particularly good sources of new information. Surprisingly, they usually reflect general knowledge that is obvious and shop-worn. It may be that they clutch to their bosoms any topics that are startlingly new so they can break the stories themselves. Or perhaps they are so busy meeting editing deadlines they have little time to reflect during an interview.

4. Academicians, when interviewed, can be a fruitful source of subject ideas. Some university authorities are engaged in consulting and, in addition, may be conducting original research in the field of the conference.

5. Interviews of consultants who are specialists in the subject matter often turn up pay dirt.

Conduct Interviews

To interview and obtain sound ideas and valid suggestions, one must be skilled at eliciting information. The interviewer must know the kinds of questions to ask and how to draw out thoughtful responses.

I have conducted one-on-one interviews as well as group interviews (two to four persons). Interviews last from 30 minutes to an hour and a half. From experience, I find these factors important in conducting interviews:

1. In advance, prepare a list of open-ended questions to serve as a springboard to get the discussion started and to fill in any gaps. The questions should fit the position, experience, and background of the person being interviewed.

   Use *what-why-how-when-where* questions. Avoid questions that will simply elicit a "yes" or "no" answer.

2. Your questions should not seek opinions, such as, "What subjects do you think should be on the program?" Rather, narrow the questions that are more likely to develop information helpful in the final selection of subjects. Here are three good questions that will elicit useful data:

   "What are the three most critical problems you face today in getting your work done more effectively?"

   "In performing your work, what one area of information would be of the greatest help to you if you knew more about it?"

   "What one person, either an individual whom you've listened to or heard about, would you listen to if it were convenient for you?"

3. Throughout an interview, keep probing beneath the pat answers that you inevitably get. "Why do you say that?" helps provoke more thoughtful responses. If you continually press to get beyond the superficial observations, the last five minutes of an interview often produce the gems of information you seek.

4. Keep your eyes and ears open during an interview to catch an idea that is not verbalized. In some cases, extraneous factors, initially unrelated to the conference theme, may stimulate your thinking and lead to a subject for the program. Here are two examples:

- In one interview, I noticed an unusually large stack of publications on the credenza behind the person with whom I was talking. I asked what the pile was, sensing the answer ahead of time. He said it was reading matter that he should scan and was waiting for the time to do so. (This conference was in a scientific field and there was much that was important to know.) Bingo! I had a subject: "The Reading Dilemma: How to keep up with information in the flood of publications in the field."

- In another interview for a different conference, I asked the interviewee what he found most and least valuable at the conferences he attended. He said one drawback was that in the evenings, if he didn't know anybody at the meeting, there was little to do but stay in his room or drink at the bar. I thought there must be others with this same problem. For the next conference, I scheduled sessions from 7:30 p.m. to 9:30 p.m. This way, those who wanted to eat early could do so and still attend the sessions, while the late eaters could have dinner after 9:30. It was my hunch that others would feel the same way as my interviewee and that there would be at least a handful of attendees who wanted something to occupy their evening. To my delight, more than 1,500 people came to the night-time sessions.

As an axiom, individuals at a conference are there for serious purposes. They want to learn. If the subjects are focused, pertinent, and properly scheduled, attendees will go to sessions and listen intently. Any lack of interest, half-hearted participation, and greater attention to play among attendees result from poor conference planning.

Clip Articles

Your research methods should also include clipping articles from publications and filing them. Throughout the year, cut out newspaper, magazine, and newsletter articles that may have a relationship—however remote—to your conference. When you begin your subject planning, review the articles; in light of your other research, see what topics may be candidates for the conference. Sometimes you may find an offbeat subject that could add a change of pace and excitement to the program. The articles might also suggest further resources.

For one engineering conference, when I reviewed the articles I had been collecting, I noticed a small newspaper story about an association of people who were interested in extraterrestrial phenomena. When I investigated, I discovered that there were engineers who were members of this association. I asked two of them if they would give a talk on UFOs, describing—in engineering terms—how these vehicles might operate in terms of speed, maneuverability, guidance, and materials. The subject was certainly offbeat. I felt that, though there might be few attendees curious enough to want to attend this session, the topic could add an unusual fillip to the program. Lo and behold, more than 500 people attended, and the subject stimulated talk throughout the conference.

Committees

If I have denigrated committees as an aid to conference planning, let me suggest a committee role in the process of developing subjects for a conference. It is not wise to give a committee the responsibility to plan the subjects. The best use of a committee's time is to have it discuss—following a prepared agenda of questions—those issues related to trends, new concepts, innovative practices, and problems in the field of the conference. The conference planner keeps notes of the committee's discussion highlights to weigh while selecting subjects.

Send Questionnaires

Select a number of attendees from last year's conference. Get a balance as to geography, function, size of operation, and product. Send a cover letter to them to solicit their help. Attach a questionnaire with questions like those which follow. Leave three or four lines beneath each question for a reply. Because these questions require thought and time, don't expect a high rate of return. But the replies you do receive are likely to contain quality answers.

For a company conference, some changes in wording may be needed.

Possible questions include the following:

1. *The most effective session at the conference I attended was: . . . because: . . .*

2. *The least effective session I attended was: . . . because: . . .*

3. *What subjects were not on the program that you would like to have heard?*

4. *What new developments in the field do you believe will have important future impact?*

5. *Could you identify one or two areas in which your organization has been working—either technical or managerial—that you believe will make a contribution to next year's program?*

The questionnaire must include blank lines so each respondent can fill in his/her name, title, address, company name, product, and telephone number should he/she offer an exciting possibility which you want to pursue.

Resist sending previous attendees any questionnaires which include a list of subjects presented at the last conference, and asking them to check those they would like to see presented again. This preconditions your respondents, and the results of the survey will provide little help toward the next program.

Often planners using this approach are inclined to suggest: *"List other topics that you would like to have on the next program."* The results of this request will be nil. Few respondents, if any, will fill in the blank lines. And what few suggestions are made will be worthless. Don't expect a non-conference planner to come up with stimulating subjects any more than you would expect anyone in a non-journalistic pursuit to create sparkling subjects for a publication.

Consult Previous Speakers

Previous speakers often have ideas for subjects. You may wish to send them a memo like the following:

M E M O R A N D U M

To: Speakers at this year's conference
From: The Program Coordinator
Subject: Next year's program

We are beginning to plan next year's conference. As a participant in this year's program, you are generally aware of the topics covered at our past conference.

Please reflect for a moment and give us your thoughts and suggestions for topics to cover at the next conference. Indicate on the enclosed self-addressed card any subjects you believe would contribute to our sessions. The subjects can relate to *[here you might list a few broad areas]*, or instead you may wish to suggest a topic in an area which has not been given sufficient coverage.

Thank you for your help in making our next program a most significant contribution to the *[industry, profession, discipline, company, business, geographic area, etc.]*.

On the self-addressed card to speakers, you might use this copy:

I suggest the following for the next conference:

TOPIC ⎯⎯⎯⎯⎯⎯⎯⎯⎯⎯⎯⎯⎯⎯⎯⎯⎯⎯⎯
Speaker ⎯⎯⎯⎯⎯⎯⎯⎯⎯⎯⎯⎯⎯⎯⎯⎯⎯⎯
Organization ⎯⎯⎯⎯⎯⎯⎯⎯⎯⎯⎯⎯⎯⎯⎯
City & State ⎯⎯⎯⎯⎯⎯⎯⎯⎯⎯⎯⎯⎯⎯⎯

TOPIC ⎯⎯⎯⎯⎯⎯⎯⎯⎯⎯⎯⎯⎯⎯⎯⎯⎯⎯⎯
Speaker ⎯⎯⎯⎯⎯⎯⎯⎯⎯⎯⎯⎯⎯⎯⎯⎯⎯⎯
Organization ⎯⎯⎯⎯⎯⎯⎯⎯⎯⎯⎯⎯⎯⎯⎯
City & State ⎯⎯⎯⎯⎯⎯⎯⎯⎯⎯⎯⎯⎯⎯⎯

Your name *(please print)* ⎯⎯⎯⎯⎯⎯⎯⎯⎯

The Subject Selection Process

When the process of subject selection begins, the conference planner should retire to a quiet environment and review all the material from the research. Any feasible subject for the conference should be numbered and recorded. At this point, conference titles are not important and value judgment should not be exercised. If in doubt, put a subject in.

This process might be likened to that of a fortune-seeker panning for precious metals. A lot of debris is sifted through to find some rare bits of gold. The idea here is that you'll sift through a lot of "debris" before you find subjects even remotely related to the conference theme. You may require only 25 subjects to fill your program. You may wind up, at this first go-through, with 200 topics. That's fine, and actually desirable. On your first cut at the 200 topics, combine, rephrase, eliminate, and sift what you believe to be the best subjects. You may end up with 50 topics on which to concentrate for further refining.

8 | Refining the Conference Program

By now you have reduced the large number of topics by a process of combining, rewording, and elimination. You now have a better-focused group of subjects, but many more than you need for the program. Your next task is to select the best of these topics, balanced according to the conference themes or tracks; audience composition; audience interests, problems, and needs; and important trends that may affect their work or careers.

Three Helpful Sources

Three sources can help the conference planner shape and sharpen the program:

1. The program committee

2. A selected number of previous conference attendees

3. One or two individuals who have good programming instincts and who know the subject area

This process can be compared to the work of a diamond cutter who starts with a dull, ragged chunk of rock. Buried within it is a precious stone. With a wire brush, the debris and extraneous material are removed. The remaining form is buffed and buffed again. Then begins the delicate work of carefully cutting and recutting, polishing and repolishing. At last a sparkling jewel emerges—the Star of India, the Hope diamond—a product appealing and attractive to many potential owners. And so the jewel of a conference can be born—laborious in its gestation and its formation, but oh-so-valuable in its worth to an audience of "buyers."

The Program Committee

The program committee can be helpful at either of two points in program conception. A committee can help once you have recorded, without value judgment, the mass of subjects gathered from various sources, or after you have exercised judgment and narrowed the huge number of original subjects to a smaller list, which is still too large for your program needs. At either point, the directions to the committee and the process to secure its contributions are the same. I like to use the committee in both stages of program conception.

To begin the process of securing the committee's contribution, send committee members your compiled list of numbered subjects. Ask them to record a rating next to every subject using the following scale:

(E)   Excellent subject

(VG)   Very good subject

(G)   Good subject

(F)   Fair subject

(P)   Poor subject

At the same time, announce the time and place of the all-day meeting at which committee members will discuss their ratings. It is important to emphasize that, in rating the subjects, the committee members should make their evaluations based on what they believe will most help the audience—not themselves. Since, typically, the program committee will be composed of the more knowledgeable people in the field, you don't want to develop a program that will be of interest primarily to these more sophisticated individuals. The presumption is that when the committee was formed, you spelled out the nature of the conference audience according to the characteristics that distinguish its composition.

At the committee meeting, go through the subjects one by one. Ask how many rated subject 1 as "E," how many "VG," and so on down the scale. If most have rated a subject as "E" or "VG," it is likely that the topic is a good one. Conversely, if most have evaluated a subject as "F" or "P," the subject should probably be

Exhibit 8.1

Dear Ms. Jones:

Your name has been selected from the hundreds (dozens, thousands) of executives (engineers, physicians, wholesalers, etc.) who attended the (name of the conference) last year. We ask your help in evaluating the subjects planned for the upcoming conference in (month, year).

Would you take five or ten minutes to rate the conference subjects listed on the attached sheet? Since the sample of names we have drawn for this evaluation is small, it is important that you respond and that your response reaches us by (date). The final program will be set and publicized based on the responses we receive.

Thank you for your kind cooperation.

P.S. A stamped and addressed envelope is attached to help speed your opinions to us.

---

dropped. Whatever the ratings, ask if anyone would like to make a further comment. Sometimes, with other insights, a subject might receive a different focus which would then make it an acceptable candidate for further study.

Most discussion in this committee meeting will cover those subjects which received widely varied ratings. Explore why members evaluated some subjects on different scales. Through the interchange, which the conference planner should lead, another angle on the subject may be uncovered that could make it appealing to all members, leading the low raters to upgrade their evaluation.

Previous Conference Attendees

Make a random selection of previous attendees and send them the list of subjects along with a personalized letter asking them to evaluate the subjects. Your letter might be like the one in Exhibit 8.1. The sheet that lists the subjects should provide instructions like those shown in Exhibit 8.2.

Exhibit 8.2

Please rate each of the subjects according to the following scale of interest to you.

1. Most interest

2. Some interest

3. Little interest

Place a rating number (1, 2, or 3) beside each subject listed.

(Your comments on any of the subjects would be most helpful, too.) Your "vote" counts! Thank you for your help.

This kind of research and letter can be adapted for both a company conference and an association conference. In the case of a company meeting, the conference planner may have to ensure the confidentiality of the replies so that comments and respondents' names will not be revealed to management.

Knowledgeable Individuals

In the many contacts that you make in conference planning, look out for one or two people—a consultant, a practitioner, or an editor—with an unusually broad understanding of the requirements of conference programming for a diverse audience as well as a sensitivity to the kinds of subjects that will appeal to your conference audience. Use their knowledge in the same way you employed the program committee. Set up appointments with them. In advance, send the same list of subjects and instructions you sent to the program committee. At your meeting, go through the ratings, subject by subject. Since you will be in a one-on-one discussion, it is easy to probe to uncover the reasoning behind the ratings.

Final Program Polishing

When you've accumulated the contributions of your three sources, it's back to the drawing board. Weigh the sources. Study your notes. Begin the refining process. Eliminate the weaker topics. Combine two related ones. Take a different focus on a subject. Narrow the list to those that you believe are the stronger ones.

Even if you've done a good job of sifting, cutting, and polishing, you will still wind up with more subjects than you need. That's good. For now, there are two additional considerations to weigh before making your final selections.

Choosing Themes or Tracks

No matter what the overall thrust of a conference, there are typically two to five major themes upon which the conference should concentrate. Deciding what these broad themes (or tracks) should be will help to give better focus to the meeting and prevent your covering the world of knowledge. For example, if the conference were in the field of economics, the themes might be an exploration of the following broad areas:

1. Economic indices

2. Short- and long-range forecasting

3. Foreign competition

Numerous related subjects could fit within each of these tracks or themes. Establishing your themes will help you decide which of the remaining subjects should be taken out and which you should retain for additional study and polishing.

Relating Subjects to the Audience

The second consideration in selecting subjects for the program is to relate them to the interests of a diverse audience. No matter whether you are planning a company conference or one sponsored by an association, do not treat the audience as a group of people with homogeneous problems, needs, and concerns. Your goal is to conceptualize a program so that most, and desirably all, of each attendee's time is spent listening to information that is pertinent to and can have an impact on the participant's working life. If the planner achieves that goal, individual attendees will not be bored.

Exhibit 8.3

	The conference matrix		
	Major themes of the conference		
	Management of Department 40% of subjects	**Training, Technology, Methodology** 50% of subjects	**Government Influence, Economy, Societal Change** 10% of subjects
Audience Composition			
Manufacturing companies	6, 10	5, 12	7
Non-profit organizations			
Government		12	
Retailing		5, 12	7
Interest to all	4, 8, 13, 14	1, 2, 3, 11	9, 15

Therefore, it is very important to consider the composition of your audience. What are the three to five major differences among the participants that will affect their interest in a subject? For a company, it might be a factor of years of experience, job responsibility, size and nature of one's territory, plant, or department. For an association, programming should consider factors such as the size of companies represented, their products or services, job responsibility, and years of experience. Of course, there are many subjects that will be interesting and appealing to all attendees.

Using a Matrix

Use a simple matrix to show graphically the degree to which a program's subjects balance according to the conference themes and audience composition. Exhibit 8.3 is an illustration of a grid developed for a meeting on human resources development. Audience members represented four different kinds of organizations. There are four fields into which the audience was divided, plus one category representing subjects that would apply for all on the horizontal columns of the grid.

Three themes on which the conference would concentrate are indicated at the tops of the vertical columns. Note that a percentage figure for each theme represents the number of subjects that should be selected for each track, since not all of these themes would hold the same importance for the attendees.

A total of 15 subjects were required for this two-day meeting, some presented concurrently. Note that some subjects, though not interesting to everyone, would interest more than one organizational category. The numbers in the matrix correspond to the subjects numbered in another listing.

It is evident from this matrix that there were no specific subjects directed to the concerns of non-profit organizations. On further reflection, the planner of this conference may want to go back to the list of subjects and refocus one or two of them for this group.

Important Principles

Whatever process you use to define the number and the subjects to include in your program, it is important to do so with these principles in mind:

1. Decide on the major themes or tracks on which to concentrate for your conference.

2. Consider the composition of your audience and the differences among them. Your selection of subjects can thus be guided to ensure that the diverse interests of attendees are reflected in your conference programming.

3. Secure many different ideas on your subject selection so that you can focus on those topics that will be most beneficial and stimulating to your audience.

4. Continue to polish and refocus your subjects until you have achieved a program that will be of maximum value, interest, and excitement to your audience.

9 | Hone Your Titles

You have developed, massaged, and refined a list of subjects for your conference. You feel secure in the selections. But will it play in Peoria? Will your "product" sell? Will conference attendees share your ardor for the subjects you have chosen?

Your most important job now is to spend time developing a specific, clear, exciting, and unambiguous title for each talk—one that will stimulate people to go to your conference.

Titles More than Cosmetics

While subjects are the muscle and marrow of the conference "body," subject titles are more than mere cosmetics. Too little attention is paid to the titling of speeches. They often are taken too lightly. They can be vague, generalized, all-encompassing, trite, or so cute that their wording is destined to dissatisfy audiences. As a result, the speaker has one idea of what the assigned title suggests, while the attendees have another.

A talk's title serves these three purposes:

1. It provides a specific and clear picture of the scope of the presentation so that the speaker and the audience both understand what the talk will cover.

2. It stimulates interest in session attendance and projects a rewarding experience.

3. It reduces the need for further copy to tell what the title really means.

If a title is unambiguous, there is less need to produce the voluminous "magazine" style of program that explains at length—with many questions still to be answered—the reason for and the importance of the subject. When the copy is too ponderous, many prospective conference attendees will not find the time to wade through it. A program set aside to be read later often is not read at all, nor is it followed by a registration.

Use Newspaper Headlines as a Guide

Consider the headlines of a newspaper as an example of and a guide to good subject titles. A skilled copywriter selects a few appropriate—and short—words to summarize the entire scope of an article in a comprehensible way. Then, as readers scan the pages of the newspaper, they can quickly and intelligently decide which stories to concentrate their time and attention on.

Do not dismiss the idea of a newspaper-headline approach to titles by reasoning that your subjects are too complex or too intellectual. Newspaper copywriters deal with stories of major breakthroughs in science, complex legislation, involved tax laws, and convoluted criminal investigations, and still write clear, succinct headlines.

Companies may believe that titles are not important for their conferences because people are required to attend. This is shortsighted thinking. Treat your audience as consumers. Properly phrased headlines for a subject can build the desired excitement and anticipatory interest in a program. Certainly for an association—dependent for a large registration on the appeal of the conference subjects—titles that are compelling and carefully defined can induce attendees to attend its conference.

Creating Titles

Here are some suggestions for creating titles that will hit the reader's "hot button." While titles should be as terse as possible, do not agonize over the length if that is necessary for clarity.

1. Use subheads (as in newspapers) to expand on the principal headline:

New research techniques test
true consumer reactions
to proposed new product:
Reduce product-intro failures

2. Begin titles with active verbs.

   Try an easy-to-use appraisal system to improve job performance

3. Use the trigger words that a reporter uses in an interview (*how, why, when, where, who*):

   How managers build in time during the
   work week to plan long range:
   Why it is critical today

Titles to Avoid

There are some kinds of titles—and, perhaps, subjects—that you should avoid.

1. Do not use a title that the reader can answer one way or the other.

   Should we encourage or discourage unions in our business?

2. A broad, generalized title lacks vigor and stimulation.

   Product planning in companies today

   I could come up with 20 to 30 different interpretations of this title. Each of them might differ from what the speaker has in mind and from what various members of the audience might infer from it.

3. Cute titles usually are just what they are—cute, and not at all compelling.

   Take the man out of management

   Often attempts at wit in titles may have meaning only for a speaker who believes he/she will excite curiosity through this approach. Since the title *per se* may have little meaning to a participant, it will often fail to draw attendees, who may have a completely different expectation of the talk's content.

4. A title that promises too much will leave attendees unrewarded.

   30 proven ways to save money in your advertising

If this talk is given in, say, 45 minutes, these "proven ways" will be covered in less than two minutes each. There will be only enough time to reel off a laundry list of ideas, resulting in information overload. This kind of subject is far more useful if it is contained in a handout given in advance. Allow the audience time to read the handout, to think about the methods, and then to ask questions. A speaker would provide more valuable information by concentrating on three or four ideas, explaining in depth the implications of their use.

5. Pie-in-the-sky titles seldom draw participants who like to think they are hard-headed and practical about their work.

The implications of the robot factory in the year 2001

While this title may seem like an exaggeration, I have seen others just as visionary. There could be a handful of dreamers who might attend a session on a similar subject. However, there are so many genuine current problems to solve, there is no need to deal with esoteric titles (or subjects) that will turn off the more typical attendee.

6. Titles that try to cover too many aspects of a subject will fall flat.

The retailer's problems with inventories,
the buyer's responsibilities,
and computer applications

Hone your titles. Keep that cutting edge sharp. Cut away excess verbiage; specify what you want your speaker to talk about.

Ask Committee to Appraise Titles

Ask your program or planning committee to appraise the titles of your sessions. This is particularly valuable if the subjects are technical and you want to be precise about the terms used and the idioms that would be acceptable.

Send each committee member a list of session titles and request that he/she review and evaluate them with the following analysis in mind.

Ask committee members to critique the language of your program titles, considering how the titles can be changed to:

- Provide a different and sharper focus on the subject
- Sound more compelling
- Read better

At the same time, announce the time and date of a committee meeting to review member suggestions. At that meeting, discuss the committee's ideas, tighten titles further, and make them even more compelling.

10 | The Sponsor's Responsibility

The conference sponsor must set guidelines for the conference planner. Time and money are wasted when a sponsor avoids setting initial parameters. The planner cannot administer the details of a conference effectively without carefully considered mandates.

The 30 questions included in this chapter are among those the planner should ask the person calling the conference—whether it is the president, marketing vice president, or association chief executive officer. Frequently, only the vaguest information or direction is provided by this person in the beginning.

By posing the right questions—and evoking lucid answers—the meeting planner has a clear track on which to run the conference. Specific questions help the conference sponsor think through, in an organized way, the areas in which decisions must be made at the outset, or at least provide some idea as to what is on the sponsor's mind. In many cases, the sponsor has not done a great deal of basic thinking, and you may find, at the time of initial discussions, that the sponsor does not have all the answers. But you will have offered an important service by flagging the matters the sponsor should attend to. You may already know the answers to some of these questions, but it is wise to get confirmation. The following questions relate primarily to a company conference, but can be adapted for an association.

Questions to Ask the Sponsor

1. Why are you holding this conference? Why is it important?

2. What do you want the attendees to know and do when they return to their jobs that is better than and different from what is true today?

3. Who will be responsible for coordinating the entire meeting, including the program, invitations, facility selection, etc.? Who will make final decisions on these matters?

4. Will there be a committee or selected persons to work with the conference planner? Who will appoint them? Will there be more than one committee for various responsibilities?

5. What ranges of experience, age, education, and sophistication in the subject matter do you expect to find among the total number of people who will attend?

6. What level of functions (job titles or responsibilities) do these people represent?

7. What conferences have been held in the past for this group?

8. From what geographical area will they come?

9. Will any people from outside the organization be invited to attend?

10. Will spouses attend?

11. How many days do you want the conference to last? Is there some flexibility in the schedule?

12. During the conference, in which time periods do you want the group to be in session: mornings, afternoons, evenings?

13. Who in the organization should be on the program as speakers?

14. Have you used outside speakers? What is your feeling about their desirability if the subject matter suggests it?

15. Are there speakers outside the organization who should be on the program because of their political importance to the organization?

16. What is the budget for the conference?

17. Will there be one billing of expenses, a charge back to departments, or individual payment?

18. How would you like the transportation for each participant handled?

19. If spouses attend, should a special program be planned for them?

20. If time is available, should we arrange for sports tournaments?

21. What type of facility do you prefer for this conference: your organization's own facility, a resort, an in-city hotel, a suburban hotel, an airport hotel, or a conference center?

22. What size facility do you prefer (under 300 rooms, 300–500, 500–1,000, or more than 1,000)?

23. For sleeping accommodations, how many suites, singles, and doubles will you require? How many overnight stays do you foresee?

24. How many group meals should we plan? Which meal(s) (breakfast, lunch, dinner)?

25. Should we provide attendees with an option to eat elsewhere rather than with the group?

26. Considering the weather, accessibility, amenities available for recreation/exercise, attractions, sightseeing, and shopping, where do you prefer we place this conference geographically?

27. Would you consider a site outside of the United States?

28. What were the weak points of your previous conferences?

29. What were the strong points?

30. How do you think the meeting should be improved?

Put the Answers in Writing

When all these questions have been answered, the conference planner has clear mandates. Answers should be put into a document with one copy each for the sponsor and the planner so that each has a ready reference to the original agreements, along with a time schedule for securing answers and making decisions.

The sponsor may have a change of mind after seeing the answers in writing. This is fine, as long as it is done early in the process. Changes in direction become costly and frustrating after plans are set in motion.

Exhibit 10.1

Schedule of Activities

Work Completion Dates and Responsibilities for Conference on Human Resource Development

[The dates listed are those by which the activity is to be completed.]

Date	Activity	Responsibility
Dec. 1	Complete selection of committtees	Gen. Chair & Chapter Presidents
Dec. 1	Send out questionnaires asking for subject suggestions	Joe Eltman
Dec. 5	Hold initial meeting of all chairpersons with general chairman	Joe Dodson
Dec. 5	Develop budget for Conference	Bob Meli
Dec. 5	Review and approve artwork for Conference letterhead	Joe Eltman
Dec. 12	Print letterheads and envelopes	Joe Eltman
Dec. 19	Select site for Conference	Carney Ives
Dec. 19	Secure mailing list for exhibitors	Tony Fitzherbert
Jan. 7	Analyze subject suggestions from questionnaires	Ben Miller
Jan. 16	Review progress and problems on Conference at meeting of entire committee	Joe Dodson
Jan. 19	Prepare and mail initial press release on Conference	Joe Eltman
Feb. 13	Visit facility selected with Program and Arrangements Committees	Ben Miller Carney Ives Bob Webb Tony Fitzherbert

Schedule of Work Completion

You are now in a position to make up a schedule and assign responsibilities to get work done. The deadlines established give you specific goals to reach within a time framework. In doing so, you will avoid the crises stemming from the pressures that can pile up as those inflexible conference dates arrive.

One approach to handling this is to write down all the activities that need to be completed. Enter dates together with who will be responsible, under your direction, to get the work done.

An abbreviated version of such a schedule is in Exhibit 10.1.

11 | Plan for Individual Attendees

Whatever its purpose, a conference can be no better than the work that goes into it. Whether you are thinking in terms of 25, 100, 300, or thousands of participants, you should be guided by the same principles and take similar steps to develop ideas and organize your event. Numbers alone should not be cause for changing—much less ignoring—sound conference principles.

A Conference's Objectives

Any conference that is well planned and properly conducted, even though it may be no more than a work-related session held periodically by an organization's management group, should achieve at least one of the following objectives—perhaps all of them:

1. It should enable attendees to carry away ideas that they want to pursue further on their own.

2. It should inspire and motivate them, back in their offices, shops, work settings, laboratories, or businesses, to act on what they have heard and learned.

3. In the case of a major three- or four-day conference for a large audience paying to attend, something further is required. Attendees are hoping for solid information on new trends and developments in their field. Those responsible for the conference's success must make sure that each session offers solutions to common problems, presents facts about some new but widely applicable technique, or explores current thinking and practice in a useful way.

4. The conference planner must see that every individual has a chance to ask questions and exchange information with fellow registrants. In short, the program must enable each person who attends the sessions to acquire greater knowledge and skill in the field covered by the conference.

As long as people come to a conference for important new information or for dealing with on-the-job problems, the conference must stand or fall on its content. If it is irrelevant to attendees' needs, or if they find it inadequate for any other reasons, they will condemn it as a waste of time. And you can be sure they will avoid repeating the experience. Or if it is a company conference they are required to attend, they will do so with a negative attitude.

Key Planning Concepts

There are eight basic concepts on which to build a productive conference. If you ignore them, you foredoom the outcome.

1. Participation is better than mere listening. An audience should be drawn into playing an active role in a conference instead of simply attending a series of lectures. People learn by sharing their impressions and experiences with others, and, eventually, applying some of their new knowledge to job problems.

2. The focus should be on the individual. No audience is a collection of homogeneous minds and backgrounds, even at a company meeting. Differences—even major ones—can be discerned in any group and should be used to guide the conference design.

3. The conference should be oriented to the hopes and goals of attendees. The objective of the sponsoring company or association must of course be considered, but the preeminence of the man or woman who attends—that primary fact of life for the conference planner—cannot be overlooked.

4. Inspiration is no substitute for lack of content. If the conference aspires only to uplift those listening, although some

motivational speakers may be desirable, the effect will be short-lived. Sessions should be mentally stimulating; minds should be at work. Participants must be forced to think about topics of substance that are pertinent to their work.

5. Treatment of subject matter should be tailored to a given audience. Speakers from outside the organization should be given an audience profile and a description of the group sponsoring the conference. Even inside speakers should be reminded of the audience's problems, needs, and concerns.

6. "What" is not enough. Your audience must know "why" and "how." When a speaker tells what was done or should be done, he/she should also say why it was done or should be done. And most important, the speaker must reveal how it was done or how to do it. When an audience is told what to do, but not why or how, it is short-changed.

7. Subjects must be treated with a narrow, laser-beam focus. Too often speakers are given topics of enormous proportion. For example, suppose a speaker is told to speak about the subject of communications or marketing. The unfortunate speaker then must try to cover every aspect of an impossible assignment. Rather, the conference planner should do the hard work before giving a speaker an assignment. The planner must identify the specific, sharp focus that will make the topic most timely and interesting for the expected audience.

8. The conference planner should know his/her audience. "I know my audience. They work for me," says the sales manager. He knows their names, their sales and incomes, and may even know their spouses. But unless someone does some extensive, firsthand research, he/she does not know what employees see as their needs and problems; those needs may be far removed from what the boss thinks they are. An audience profile, developed from research in the field, should be created to guide the conference planner. Thinking that comes from the boss's ivory tower seldom approaches the realness of the audience's needs and problems.

12 | The Virus of Boredom

It is true that you cannot expect to please everyone all the time. This is a fact to keep in mind when making plans for a conference. Trying to come up with a program that will suit everyone in the audience is every planner's goal; it is also a sure road to frustration, depression, and resentment. However, that goal still should guide your planning.

The diversity of the average conference audience is a universal problem. The audience members may be of the same profession, may work at much the same sort of job, and may be employed by similar organizations. They may deal with similar products or work on comparable projects. They may even be equally familiar with the conference's announced subject matter. However, their thresholds of boredom may vary widely. Most of all, they will differ in the ease with which they can grasp and retain new, sometimes sophisticated knowledge.

Throughout your conference, therefore, you can expect to hear conflicting reactions, often inspired by the same presentation. The challenge is to meet the needs of as much of your audience as possible without basking unduly in praise or worrying excessively about criticism. There is something unhealthy about the extreme need for praise—or worse, the belief that it should be forthcoming, and, if it is not, there must be something wrong. Something may be wrong, but it may well be the conference planner's own attitude and perceptions. Or it could be the virus that lurks in the air of most conferences.

Amateur conference planners tend to forget a basic characteristic of human beings who must sit in a conference for an entire morning or afternoon with perhaps only two short breaks. They easily succumb to the virus of boredom.

Basically, they do so because of the inadequacies of amateur speakers, who may account for 95 percent of the typical program.

Audience Concentration Is Limited

With the best of will, an audience finds it difficult to concentrate for more than 20 to 25 minutes on what these individuals have to say. Unlike professional speakers, amateurs cannot hold their listeners much longer. And if they read their speeches rather than maintain eye contact with the audience, even 20 minutes may seem like hours.

Furthermore, people's minds wander when they have to listen attentively to someone talking at the average rate of 125 words a minute, while they can listen at a rate of four times that speed. Then, too, most amateur speakers do not have enough experience to be at ease in front of a large group and develop a style that will captivate its members, sometimes in spite of themselves. Worse, amateur speakers have never been forced by a tough-minded conference planner to do a real job of focusing on the specifics of a topic. They cling, instead, to the easy generalities that require little or no thought and are resented by audiences as a waste of high-priced listening time.

Most important is the fact that the average conference audience is made up of people of action. Yet conference speakers, in effect, are asking them to become passive hearers and learners. This psychological switch is a difficult one, so the average group rapidly becomes uneasy. Moreover, since such restlessness is contagious, even the best-planned presentations may falter.

Antidotes to the Virus of Boredom

Luckily, there are antidotes to the viruses of dullness and boredom in the variety of conference design ideas available to planners. Six examples will suggest others that you can develop or can adapt when you come upon them. It is important to be sensitive to the need for variety and to be alert to other examples used outside your organization. Here are some alternatives to straight speeches:

1. Limit talks to five minutes, but expand the accompanying discussion period. The need to be brief will force the speaker to concentrate on essentials. Such a setup helps a speaker who is loaded with information and experience, but who

tends to talk in a monotone because of nervousness. In a free-wheeling discussion, he/she can relax, be more animated, and keep the audience interested.

2. Instead of a "real talk," ask the speaker to submit six questions which you will have a chairperson ask. This will stimulate questions from the audience as well and turn what could be a dull session into a spirited exchange. Generally, speakers are more at ease answering questions than giving formal talks.

3. As an alternative, give each of the six questions to different members of the audience to ask. This will quickly trigger the desired discussion and keep it moving. Those given one of the six questions should be advised not to ask it if members of the audience are already actively asking questions. The original questions are passed out to get a discussion going and to fill voids when questions stop coming.

4. Select two persons and ask each to talk for five or ten minutes on a different side of a controversial issue. Afterward, have them discuss the subject under the direction of a skilled moderator.

5. Rehearse a speaker beforehand and then have professionals videotape the results. Professionals can create visual effects that will add novelty to a session when you offer a video as a change of pace at your conference. However, a videotaped speaker should be present to answer questions after the videotape is shown. In fact, the introduction of the live speaker after the videotape can be made dramatic with as simple an effect as a following spotlight as the speaker steps from the audience or from behind a curtain.

6. Remember to break your audience into smaller groups from time to time. Seat them at round or rectangular tables to form discussion groups. Your objective should be to involve and affect every member of your audience. You must therefore provide every possible opportunity for active, continual participation.

Because no single meeting technique will be equally effective with all subject matter or with every individual present, you should use a variety of formats. In short, use a little ingenuity. Break away from potentially boring conference patterns, and, in the process, compensate for those speakers who are leaders in their fields but less-than-stimulating platform performers.

13 How to Select and Invite Speakers

An analogy can be drawn between the speakers at a conference and the actors in a play. No matter how good a play's script is, unless the actors can bring it to life and deliver the lines dramatically, the play will fail.

No matter how brilliantly the conference program subjects are conceived, if the speakers do not interpret and present those topics well, the conference will not succeed. With some apology for the undistinguished word of comparison, there is some truth expressed by one of the old bromides in the computer field: it is GIGO (garbage in, garbage out).

So if your conference is to achieve maximum impact, you must concentrate on the sole core of implementors in the conference learning process—the speakers. Take these three critical steps of organization and execution to ensure your speakers' competence and meaningful contribution:

1. Identify and gather the names of the finest group of potential speakers culled from a variety of sources.

2. Carefully evaluate this cadre to select those who will best deliver on the subjects you have selected.

3. Instruct them completely once they have accepted your invitation to speak. Provide them with information on what your research shows the audience wants to know. Continually work with them on their presentations.

Four Categories of Speakers

First, it is helpful to put into perspective the sources and types of speakers from which you can make your choices. There are essentially four categories from which to select speakers. A company hosting a conference will draw most of its speakers, if not all of them, from within the organization—the practitioner category. However, to add a change of pace to the program and inject other points of view, use speakers from outside the firm for some portion of the conference.

Associations, on the other hand, will choose speakers from four categories (with some overlap among them), including industry practitioners, academics, outside "experts," and ceremonial or political speakers.

Industry Practitioners

These are the people on the firing line. They analyze and solve real problems; adapt and introduce new programs, procedures, and practices; and make budgets and control costs.

They are not theorists. They speak from experience. They come from a milieu in which they handle people daily, direct activities, face crises, and look for a bottom line in the tough, competitive world of business.

Practitioners are very desirable speakers on a program. Their knowledge is communicated from a realistic, hands-on orientation. Unfortunately, the typical association conference does not use many practitioners, because they are busy, hard to get, and perhaps harder to identify. Associations tend to invite consultants who are much more likely to accept an invitation.

Academics

Other speakers come from university and college campuses. Many professors and instructors do consulting work on the side. If they do, they have some familiarity with business life. In some instances, professors have gained the practical insights of business from having worked in a company before deciding to make a career switch to academia.

Because teachers make their living through oral communication, they offer the advantage of being able to articulate ideas with clarity and forcefulness. Yet one should be cautious in the use of some college professors. The time they have spent in the teaching profession often orients their communication style to too basic a lecture form. This format and content, replete with theories, formulae, and esoteric principles, may not be suitable for an audience accustomed to a practical, hands-on approach.

Outside "Experts"

The three groups included in this category are prominent names, consultants or suppliers, and professional speakers.

Prominent Names. These individuals are recognizable either because their names are in the headlines or they are CEOs of well-known companies. Their presence on a program is calculated to draw attendees. They make the audience think that a conference must be important if it can attract such a speaker to its program. Back home, an individual, with a degree of pride, can tell friends, "I heard 'so and so' and he/she said . . ."

In the case of the "name" speaker, it doesn't matter that the speech probably will have been written for him/her by someone else, or given before, or already published in a newspaper interview.

For one conference that I planned, I secured the president of a well-known company. When the time came to give his talk, he strode to the lectern, set down his speech, arranged his glasses, and began to read his talk word for word. About the sixth page down, he stopped, took off his glasses, looked out at the audience, and said, "You know something. This is a darn good speech." He then calmly put his glasses back on and merrily went about reading the rest of his talk. Unfortunately, you can't get Mr. Big Name to a rehearsal where you might diplomatically point out that his style of delivery could be enhanced.

If the "name" speaker has been on the lecture circuit before, he/she is likely to be represented by a lecture bureau. There will be a substantial cost to have that name on your program. I have never felt that this type of paid speaker is worth the enormous expenditure for the value which will be derived from his/her presence. Spend the money to build a solid, informative conference—not on the window dressing these speakers provide. However, they are easy to get if you're willing to pay the price. I question the conventional wisdom that they add lustre and appeal to a conference and are worth the amount of money you pay to get them.

Consultants or Suppliers. Association conferences frequently use this type of speaker, to the detriment of conference integrity. These speakers certainly are knowledgeable and smart. They also are eager to accept your invitation. This is why so many associations, with so many speakers to secure, turn to the warm body who will say "yes" immediately to an invitation to appear on the program. However, I don't think it is a good idea to inundate a conference with this category of speaker.

One complaint that I have heard for years from conference registrants is that the speakers who are consultants or suppliers have a captive audience of potential buyers of their services or products. Too frequently, attendees say, these speakers will subtly or not-so-diplomatically introduce "pitches" for their wares. That sentiment may be unfair, but the attitude prevails.

Consultants or suppliers, chosen judiciously and sprinkled through a program, can make significant contributions to a conference and can be an important asset.

Professional Speakers. There is a large group of motivational and humorous speakers who spend all of their time giving talks. That is their business. They are excellent, stimulating, and exciting to listen to, and they can hold an audience's attention for a long time.

They provide a good change of pace in a program. These speakers are thoroughly professional—on time, no big egos, willing to cooperate in every way, eager to please—and they deliver. Some, if asked and briefed in advance, will tailor parts of their talks to the special needs of your conference.

While these professionals charge a fee, it is not as outrageous as those charged by some "name" speakers. Many are represented by a lecture bureau. If you don't have a specific speaker in mind, these bureaus have a list of them and can help you make a selection.

Ceremonial or Political Speakers

This category of speaker is typically used at the opening of a conference. For a company meeting, the opening talks will be given

by a predictable group of speakers—ranging from top management, to department heads, to specialists. There may be a few
speakers who, for "political" reasons, may be asked to give a talk.
The opening of the company conference usually is traditional.

It is the association convention where the problem lies. Often,
the convention opens with a parade of personalities who have
some role to play in the association or with the conference itself. It
is here that the program starts to drag, grow boring, and become
unnecessarily downbeat. I was at a conference where eight such
speakers made a talk, including the association president, association staff head, chair of the program committee, chair of the social committee, etc. Of the eight, six opened their remarks with,
"Welcome to the . . . Convention!" Oh, how tired that phrase becomes after an hour.

The professional conference planner must exercise authority,
tact, and control to prevent this kind of waste. Never forget that
the planner's first duty is to the registrants and to what will make
the conference memorable and productive for them.

I was invited to Washington, D.C., during the Carter administration and was asked if I would help the White House staff plan
its Conference on Families. As a pro bono contribution, I spent
time with the staff discussing the one-day conference. Whatever
one's view of President Carter, it is generally agreed that he is not
a powerful speaker. I pointed out to the staff that his presence on
the program was important as a ceremonial gesture. It showed
the President's support for the aims of the conference. But that
endorsement could as well be done in a three- to five-minute
opening statement. It could be presented on closed-circuit TV or
by playing a pre-recorded tape. Their initial plan was to have the
President give a 45-minute opening presentation.

I felt that a 45-minute talk at the beginning of this conference
would be a mistake from which the conference would take quite a
while to recover.

For the ceremonial opening of another conference, I suggested that the chairperson give a flattering introduction to each
of the speakers to be recognized. The speakers would be placed in
a prominent position in the room and, when introduced, would
stand to acknowledge the applause. This would be supplemented
with slides and music to make it a little more dramatic. The total
time actually taken was less than ten minutes.

Research for Speakers

identifying and gathering names of potential speakers should go on all year. If you were to wait until the conference was upon you to think about speakers, the deadlines and pressures would build up. The conference date would rapidly approach, forcing the planner to simply enlist whoever could make the date and would be willing to talk. There would be little regard for competency or even appropriateness.

When you assemble a list of possible speakers, use the same approach I suggested for accumulating subjects from your reading throughout the year. Using the following four suggestions, put the names you gather into a folder for later examination.

1. Cut out or take careful notes on articles and names from magazines, newspapers, and books that you read. If you find material that is stimulating and fresh and offers new ideas, cut it out or write down the name of the author and his/her affiliation. In some cases, a reporter writing the story will identify a company that is doing something unusual, but will leave out the name of the person responsible for the work. If you are still interested at a later date, you can always contact the company to learn who has the most information about the development.

   In one conference, I wanted to get a speaker on a specialized subject. I had two names, but they had been overused. Also, I discovered that they typically presented talks that were formula-oriented and theoretical.

   I went to the library and got out books on the subject. The two names that I had were well represented. However, as I browsed through the books I found that they would be barely intelligible to a layman. But I found another book on the same subject that was written in a language I could understand and also seemed to have many practical ideas for a business audience. I tracked down this author at an office in New York City. I met with him and found that he was stimulating, knowledgeable, and articulate. I invited him to give a talk at the conference. He was a smash and I have invited him to speak on several other occasions. Incidentally, after 20 years, I maintain a friendship with this remarkable man.

2. Tap your program committee for names of speakers they have heard. Perhaps they can identify individuals in their own organizations.

3. If an association has chapters, use the chapter resources. While planning a national conference for an association, I wrote to the presidents of several chapters. I asked each to send me one or two names of speakers who presented exceptionally good talks at one of their chapter meetings. I received more than two dozen names, affiliations, and talk titles from this approach.

4. In the questionnaire sent to previous registrants asking for subject suggestions, include a question such as: *"Have you heard a speaker whose knowledge and presentation ability impressed you? Yes ___ No ___ . If yes, please indicate the speaker's name, subject, and affiliation. Thanks!"*

When you begin the process of matching speaker to subject, you will find, in going back to your file, a surprising number who can fit into your program. Your planning is well underway if you do this valuable ongoing search for competent speakers.

Evaluate Before Inviting Speakers

The evaluation process is not easy. But it is worth the effort to fill your conference with a great number of competent presenters. Your aim is not only to find speakers who know the subject area, but ones who can present ideas effectively. So it is desirable to develop a process that can help you, as best you can, to check on the qualifications of a speaker before inviting him/her to be on your program.

One approach I have used is to organize a committee of evaluators throughout the country. I explain their responsibilities to them before obtaining their agreement to help. They virtually always agree. From time to time, I send them the names of potential speakers located in their area. Without contacting the individuals, the evaluators will engage their own networks of people—who may know and may have heard the speakers—to evaluate them. It is amazing how well this process has worked for me. It has enabled me to drop some speakers who were on my original list but who would have bombed on the program. I was forewarned by one or more evaluators in the network.

Another successful evaluation practice involves calling a person I know who is a co-worker of a recommended speaker. I ask my acquaintance whether he/she has ever heard the possible invitee give a talk. If not, without contacting the recommended speaker, my acquaintance checks around the company to see if anyone else might have listened to the individual give a talk.

Of course this is a lot of work. Some conference planners may throw up their hands and, understandably, feel they cannot find the time to go through all this trouble. But if your objective is to produce a conference that will be of greatest benefit to an audience and make the conference time most productive, this evaluation step is essential. If you do less, you expose your audience to a pallid, uneven, less-than-valuable conference that is unfortunately characteristic of many programs today.

Your Invitation to Speakers

When you issue the initial invitation to a speaker, it is important to provide only key facts about the conference. Include enough facts about the nature of the talk desired so the speaker will form an accurate perception of it. In addition, include pertinent administrative data. Do not burden the prospect with excessive detail that may keep him/her from taking the time to read your invitation immediately. You can send complete details later, anyway, if the prospect accepts your invitation to speak.

Here is a list of what to include in the first contact (adjust for a company conference):

1. Dates of the conference.

2. Place where the conference will be held, including city and state.

3. Date and time of talk.

4. Length of talk and total timing of talk and discussion period.

5. If anyone else is in the same session, what other talks will be given and by whom, if known.

6. The sponsor (if not known, the kind of organization sponsoring the conference).

7. The composition of the audience (if not evident).

8. Compensation arrangements (expenses, honorarium, no charges).

9. The title and scope of the talk you want the person to give.

Develop a Scope for Every Talk

It is incumbent on a professional planner to develop a scope for every talk on the program. In this way, there will be far less misunderstanding about what you want an individual to cover. If the prospect balks or does not believe he/she can deliver a talk on a topic, now is the time to know—not when the person is on the platform and giving a speech you did not expect to hear.

Here is an example of the information to supply:

Subject—*"What Kind of Tests Will Give Valid Learning Results in a Training Class?"*

Scope—*"Review the typical tests administered during or at the end of a training program and evaluate the advantages and disadvantages of each as a predictor of what a participant has learned. What can be done to improve their validity?"*

How to Extend Invitations

There are three ways invitations generally are conveyed: by letter, by phone, and through a second party.

By Letter. This approach is used often. The letter should contain the kind of information, described earlier, to be put into the initial invitation. To shorten the letter, it is a good idea to include an attractive printed card or sheet which presents some of the uniform information that all speakers should have. Include a date by which you would like a reply. I normally give a week to ten days, depending on the location of the speaker. If you have not heard by the deadline, call the speaker. Always retain control. If you wait for someone to reply, you may get hung up for a long time and never get an answer. The person might have moved to another organization, retired, gone on an overseas assignment, been lazy, or not received the invitation.

By Phone. This is the method I prefer. It takes only a few minutes to discuss the talk with a prospect. You can answer questions and clarify points at once. It is easier to establish whether this person has an understanding of the topic you want him/her to cover. There is little delay in getting a "yes" or "no," or "let me think about it." A follow-up letter may be necessary, but even if it is, you are far ahead of the game with this personal contact and review. Then, too, it is easier to set the deadline for a reply either by asking the individual when you can expect an answer or by setting the time for a reply.

Using a Second Party. This other person could be the public relations director of a company which employs a person you want to invite. This second party can help you assess the likelihood of securing the prospect you want and, if possible, might then contact the potential speaker. Particularly if you are going after a CEO, a good point of entry is often the public relations department.

In another approach, I enlist the help of a member of my program committee who is friendly with a potential speaker—perhaps a golfing friend, a buyer from the individual's company, or a close colleague. I provide the committee member with all the pertinent information and ask him/her to make a personal contact. If you use this method, you have a good chance of securing an acceptance, depending upon how heavily your friend wants to lean on the executive and the leverage exerted. I have also used this strategy with someone I know who works in the same company, asking that person to contact the potential speaker on my behalf.

If you use a second party to help, be specific and thorough with the information you provide—in writing. This way, it is less likely that the person acting as go-between will filter your verbal instructions and communicate your desires incorrectly.

For one conference, I wanted to secure a person who had figured prominently in the news for his views on a particular issue. I called a friend in the individual's organization. I learned the point of contact was not the public relations department but this person's assistant. I called the assistant and explained in detail the importance of the conference, its audience, and what we wanted the speech to cover. I sent a confirming letter.

At this point, my invitee was receiving, I was told, 25 invitations a week and was able to accept, perhaps, one a month. Unfortunately, our conference was not accepted because of a scheduling conflict. But when I later talked with the assistant, he said that of the last 50 invitations only two—one of which was ours—provided sufficiently pointed information so that an intelligent decision could be made about acceptance. The other 48, he said, were vague, general, and brief. The assistant inferred that the organizations sending them were less interested in content and simply wanted a drawing-card name on the program.

Be Open to Change

At times you may find that a speaker you want is willing to talk but would like to speak on another topic or take a different focus on the selected subject. If the speaker's preferred subject is relevant to your conference, be flexible. Make a revision in your program. Be constantly alert for ways to sharpen the meeting. Never cast the program in concrete to the degree that no improvement is possible.

Enlisting Good Speakers Takes Time

Possible speakers who have both special knowledge or affiliation and speaking skills—an essential, hard-to-find combination—are always in demand and must be approached early. Even so, many will be unavailable. You may need months of lead time to fill your program with people who have real drawing power.

Many planners feel that at least one "name" speaker—the sort of individual who is known not just to the specialist, but to any educated person—is essential to the appeal of the typically large, potentially successful conference. But a president of a prominent Fortune 500 corporation—like a much-televised political figure—probably receives five to ten such invitations a week. This executive seldom is even aware of the invitations, which are screened routinely by a secretary, an assistant, or the public relations department.

Improving the Odds of Acceptance

Obviously, the president of a major corporation, or another national figure, is going to accept very few invitations—possibly no more than two or three over a period of months. So the odds that you will be lucky are not good. However, they can be improved if: (1) someone in your own organization is actually acquainted with the person you are trying to enlist as a speaker—or knows someone who is; (2) one or more companies with which you can claim any close connection are customers of the invitee's firm; or, as a last resort, (3) you can arrange to send a persuasive individual or a delegation to visit the public relations director of the person's company to extend your invitation.

Satisfactory speakers sometimes are available through lecture bureaus listed in classified telephone directories. Local groups that use their services—such as the Chamber of Commerce, Kiwanis, Rotary, and the like—may be able to recommend specific organizations or individuals who represent professional speakers.

Remember, however, that most professional speakers address themselves to the general public. They have a few set talks, embodying the more widely accepted truths, from which you are asked to pick.

On the other hand, college and university faculties—also excellent sources of speakers—frequently can suggest willing professors who may agree to study your operation in some depth and build a talk around it. Their fees will depend on the amount of study and preparation time they require.

Speaking Ability Has the Edge

Which is more important in a speaker: special knowledge and expertise in a given area, or speaking ability, the know-how needed to interest an audience in one's topic and hold that interest for 25 or 30 minutes? As long as subject matter is at least adequate, speaking ability has the edge. Not every featured individual on a program has to make a formal presentation, however. Keep in mind that the individual with poor speaking skills can be made more comfortable in an informal format of questions and answers.

14 | Role of the Session Chairperson

The skilled chairperson can add an extra dimension to a conference. Will the session function traditionally with the chair sitting in a passive capacity, carrying out minimum administrative responsibilities? Or will there be a dynamism to the session through the firm direction of the chairperson serving as a catalyst, oiling the wheels of the program, ensuring that it flows smoothly and effectively toward an exciting conclusion? The chairperson, in effect, is the representative of the audience. As such, he/she should make certain that the session is maximally responsive and is sensitive to the needs and interests of the attendees.

The role of chairperson is often underestimated by conference planners. The wrong people can be selected for the wrong reasons. Simply being charming or outgoing is not qualification enough. The chairperson must understand the process of group dynamics—what forces are at work in a group—and use the tested "tools" that help groups function with success.

A conference will have many chairpersons. One will open the conference and set the style and pace. Others will chair individual sessions, often held concurrently.

The Chairperson's Tasks

The chairperson of a conference session has these tasks to perform:

1. Greet those present.

2. Comment on the timeliness and crucial nature of the material to be covered and the challenge it represents.

3. Outline the objectives of the session and what conferees should expect to get out of the experience.

4. Provide details of the operation of the conference. These details may include:

- The overall schedule.

- When audience participation will be welcomed and what procedure will be followed.

- Any plans for distributing copies of talks, outlines, or audiotapes.

- The system for paging registrants or delivering messages.

- The whereabouts of telephones, restrooms, and other facilities.

   If these details are not covered by the chairperson, they should be included in the handout material to help registrants adjust quickly to the conference's routine.

5. Remind listeners of the first topic and its significance to the conference's goal.

6. Introduce the first speaker with short biographical notes to indicate the speaker's qualifications to handle the subject. (Try not to read the word-for-word biography supplied by the speaker, but pick out a few salient points and present them in your own words.)

7. After the talk, summarize it briefly and point out its highlights.

8. Open the session to questions from the audience. Q&A portions of the conference often are the most important and most rewarding for both speakers and attendees. These segments help the audience to grasp the significance of the subject, clarify ideas, find solutions to problems, and gain new insights.

9. Rephrase a question if it is unclear, or restate barely audible questions. It is a good practice to repeat every oral question to make sure everyone hears it. It also gives the speaker an extra few seconds to ponder the best answer.

10. Probe with an additional question if a speaker's answer is incomplete or off the subject. The chair also should occasionally offer additional ideas if he/she has pertinent comments to add which will broaden the thinking on a subject.

11. Maintain the planned schedule. The clear sign of professionalism for all sessions is to open and close on time. The chairperson must not allow any speakers to go past the time allotted. Nor can the chairperson permit questions to run past the session's planned closing. (It is always better to have to close off questions when the "pot is boiling" than to have to keep "stoking the furnace" to get the audience to participate.)

Leading Small Group Discussions

If the design of your conference involves dividing the larger audience into separate rooms and smaller groups of perhaps 10–30 persons, the chairpersons serve a different role: they become discussion leaders.

The chairperson of a small, informal group discussion has a few added challenges to deal with: the diverse personalities that make up every small group and the fact that each one should participate to further the goal of the session.

To create a conducive environment for interaction, the chairperson should do the following:

1. Set boldly lettered name signs in front of each participant.

2. Allow each participant to introduce himself/herself by name, job or title, organization, and experience in the subject to be covered or opinions on the topic. Three or four sentences should be enough for each group member. (Politely but firmly scotch the grandstander who is inclined to make a speech when given the floor for this introduction period.) This opening period allows the group to recognize the resources available.

3. Query the group about the topic: how broadly or narrowly do group members want to pursue it? Get an agreement on an objective for the session. There is little value in discussing

something that nobody really cares about or in foreclosing on a subject of great interest to all attending.

4. Pose an opening question for group participation related to the project assigned by the session chair. Try to get a contribution from everyone in the group. For example, ask, "What is the greatest threat to the profession today?"

5. To draw in a quiet member of the group, state the person's name first, and then ask the person about his/her experience with the matter under discussion. Everyone can talk about his/her experience without feeling threatened. Even if the questioned group member says he/she never had the experience or a problem in the area discussed, that in itself could lead to further discussion. "Tell us, Jim, how did you avoid it?" might be a good follow-up question. By stating his/her name first, you alert the questioned person to listen carefully.

6. From time to time ask for a group consensus: "Do you all agree that . . . ?" or "Would someone want to put it another way?"

7. Frequently, summarize what has been discussed and agreed upon.

8. Make sure that everyone understands what is being asked or stated during the session. If you detect some cloudy statements, ask the group member if he/she could clarify. "Linda, do you mean that . . . ?" or "Henry, do I understand that you would . . . ?"

9. Do not let generalizations go unchallenged: "Lee, how do you know?" or "Where did you hear that?"

10. Resist, as a chairperson, the role of teacher or oracle. Your job is to spur discussion rather than proffer opinions or bits of wisdom. Occasionally, however, you can intercede with a comment to revitalize discussion. While you may be well-versed in the subject, your task is to ensure a flow of discussion, keeping it on track and on time for a closing summary.

11. Prevent monopoly of the floor by one person. When the long-winded talker takes a breath, ask the group, "Would someone like to comment on Willard's statement?" Let the group,

rather than you, control a member. You become the teacher when you chastise, and eclipse the free-flowing discussion.

12. Seek positive suggestions rather than let the discussion be relegated to a griping session. Try turning negatives into positives: "Mary, what good things might grow out of this situation?"

13. When there are many points on both sides of a question, list them on a blackboard or flip chart. Often when the group can see the items under the "pros" and "cons" columns, it directs discussions toward more productive ends.

14. Try to stimulate opposing ideas or statements. Encourage controversy. It is the grist that grinds down the loose ideas and produces refined thought.

15. Let the group, rather than you, evaluate ideas. Say, "What do you think of Sam's idea?" rather than "That's a good idea, Sam."

16. If the discussion is getting sidetracked, ask the group: "Is this discussion related to our objective for this session?" Let the group members get back to the subject; do not act as disciplinarian.

17. If you have not appointed someone to take notes on ideas discussed or opinions expressed—always a good idea—make some notes for yourself. This allows you to produce a balanced summary at the close of the session.

    In your note-taking, it is a good idea to list ideas and suggestions with the names of the persons who offered them. In your final summary, give credit to the contributors as you review what was discussed. For example, you might say, "Frank suggests that there are four ways to save time in covering a territory. Susan describes how to get ideas approved upstairs. Alan gives us three cautions in dealing with the computer whizzes."

Always Instruct Chairpersons

If you are the conference planner, make sure to give instructions, such as the foregoing, to your session chairpersons so they know what is expected of them. You can add to, subtract from, or alter the advice offered here, but do put into writing your instructions stating how a chairperson should perform.

It is wise to have a pre-conference briefing of chairpersons. It need only take 30 to 40 minutes. You might let them role-play situations that will surely arise involving the non-stop talker, the silent sulker, the jokester, and the positives (the clarifier, the challenger, the experienced hand, and the statistics maven).

Chairpersons need guidelines. Few, if any, are pros at the job of leading group discussions. Most of them do well, however, when they are given the "tricks of the trade" and learn exactly what their role should be.

15 | Instructions for Speakers

After a speaker has agreed to take part in a program, the immediate and subsequent communications should concentrate on the talk. In the next letter, send only the administrative details necessary at this early stage of conference development.

The Roles a Conference Planner Plays

Before we identify the material to send to a speaker, consider the roles a professional conference planner plays in three contexts. Thinking in these terms, the planner can help the speaker present a cogent, stimulating, and useful speech. In examining the following three areas—master builder, theatrical director, and magazine editor—focus on the responsibilities they represent rather than get hung up on the arbitrary titles I use.

Master Builder

You have carefully built a structure (the conference). The details of each part of the program should now be turned over to a group of "architects" (your speakers). They will be incorporating all the specifications you have provided into each of their creative monuments. Together, they become part of the whole "building." To the degree your guidelines are specific and clear, they will find it easier to help strengthen the entire edifice.

Theatrical Director

In this capacity, the conference planner is like a director of a play, blending and choreographing the action of the actors (speakers) into a totally absorbing drama. To do so, urge your speakers to be innovative in the approach taken to present their ideas. Let your own creative juices flow in thinking of ways that individual talks, and particularly your principal session, can be presented in unconventional designs. Let me give two examples.

Role Play on TV. At a marketing conference, one of the main sessions dealt with market research techniques to use to elicit opinions on new products. Through perceptive in-depth interviews with potential customers, we planned to show how to read between the lines of their comments and evaluate what customers really thought rather than what they said.

I gathered a group of four skilled and experienced interviewers for a role-play demonstration. They happened to be practicing psychologists. The ballroom in which we held the conference had a stage at one end. On the stage was a large screen. In a room next to the ballroom, we set up two TV cameras which would record the action and project it onto the large screen set up on the ballroom stage. The projected images were large so that the entire audience could see them clearly.

We arranged easy chairs in the room next door for the psychologist-actors to sit on. Two of the psychologists, the interviewers, played marketers; the other two, the interviewees, played consumers. The psychologist-actors had studied the scripts we had prepared and given to them in advance. The scripts covered the various aspects of the product on which we wanted data, such as how the product could be used.

The session chairperson stood on the stage. His words were also scripted. He introduced the session and explained that three role plays would be projected onto the screen. What he didn't say was that the cameras would project the action live from the next room.

At the end of each role play, the chairperson pointed out why the interviewers had asked particular questions, how a certain kind of probing helped to garner additional information, and what marketers could conclude when they analyzed the "consumers'" answers.

We went through three role plays in this way. At the end of the third, the four "actors" stepped out of their roles in the next room and dramatically appeared on the stage. The psychologists then answered audience questions pertaining to what the interviewees had and hadn't said—and how marketers could read between the lines.

Slides of the Speakers. At another conference, we planned a major session on the economy and the forecasts of business for the coming year. The approach we took was to select five bellwether products and a spokesperson for each company manufacturing that basic product. We wanted to know what the spokesperson thought would happen to the company's sales in the next year, what the key factors were that led to the forecast, and what negative conditions might affect the projections. To add lustre to the program, we decided to invite the presidents of the companies manufacturing the bellwether products to make the presentations.

However, in order to ensure acceptances, we tried a different design. We would interview each president by telephone. Obviously, we could make the phone hook-up anywhere the presidents happened to be, following the time schedule we had set. In one case, the CEO was in California and we phoned him at home. Ahead of time, I asked each person who accepted—all did and were intrigued with the idea—to send me 12 slides of himself/herself in different postures on the phone.

On the day of the conference, the stage was arranged to seat a chairperson and, on each side of the stage, a co-chair at a desk with a phone. Offstage were technicians from the telephone company who put through the calls to the presidents in the sequence set, patched in the conversations to the audio system of the hotel, and controlled the voice volume.

The chair introduced the session arrangement. In the meantime, the co-chair on the right had the first president holding on the line. When the chair introduced the initial speaker, a spotlight was turned to the right, the volume was turned up, and the co-chair greeted the first president, who then gave the first ten-minute talk over the phone. At intervals during the speech, the different telephone-in-hand slides of the speaker that we had collected in advance were projected on the screen. In this manner, the action moved from one side of the stage to the other until all five presidents had delivered their presentations.

If you have a large number of speakers on a program, you can't create a special design for each one. But try to be innovative in the major sessions, at least.

Magazine Editor

When playing this role, the planner should examine each talk when it is written, as an editor does for the articles in a magazine. Unlike a magazine editor, however, the planner has an irrevocable deadline and cannot reschedule the "publication" of a talk.

To accomplish this editorial function, it is necessary to secure something in written form from everyone on the program—a summary of a talk, the full text, or a detailed outline.

Not every speaker will cooperate. But for those who do—and most will—you will have a check on how well the talks will serve the needs of the audience.

The Company Conference

For a company conference, the conference planner must take an active role, combining all the skills needed to execute the three roles outlined above.

Sit with each speaker. Talk about content. Discuss innovative ways to present the information dramatically. At intervals, review the material being developed to see how it fits into the concept of the meeting. Revise. Modify. Continue to improve the material until it meshes neatly in a program that will provide maximum stimulation and value to your audience. It will not happen automatically. In a company conference, you have an added advantage in that you can get your speakers to rehearse talks and, if desired, to videotape presentations for review.

Plan for Short Talks

Because a formal conference talk lasting more than 25 minutes can be difficult for anyone except a professional speaker to give, the best plan is to schedule short talks. Unfortunately, speakers tend to become long-winded, not only when they get carried away by their own eloquence, but also when—lacking self-discipline—they delay preparation until the last minute, fail to think through their material, and are forced to improvise. That is why the experienced conference planner discusses the scope of each talk with the speaker (the scope should not be so broad as to produce generalities) and suggests five or six key issues or questions to help the speaker develop the talk.

What to Send a Speaker Who Accepts

The two key pieces of information to send to each speaker after he/she accepts are:

1. The scope of the talk and a few representative questions or issues to cover in the talk.

2. Any ideas you may have about interesting ways to present the talk. Your ideas might best be discussed first on the phone and then confirmed in your letter.

The Speaker Folder

I put the above information, including a summary of other details previously discussed, into a folder with the name of the conference and the words "Your Part of the Program" printed on the cover. The speaker can use the two inside pockets to store information you send so that all relevant material about the conference is in one place. The special folder conveys a quality image and a mark of professionalism in conference management.

On the first page in the folder, the following information is printed because it is the same for all speakers for a specific conference:

- Dates of the conference

- Conference site (city and hotel)

- Sponsoring organization (with explanation of its purpose, if not generally known)

- What industries, professional fields, or disciplines will be represented

- Range of functions and experience of attendees

On the next page, these headings are printed (with specifics typed in for each speaker):

- *Title of your talk:*

- *Date and time of your talk:*

- *Length of talk and discussion period:*

- *Title of your session (and other talks in the session, if any):*

- *Location in which you will give talk:*

- *Scope of your talk:*

- ***Examples of questions or issues to be covered in your presentation:*** *Please use these thoughts as idea stimulators, as recommendations, and as a framework for developing your speech. Add to or refocus them to make your talk of greatest value to the audience.* [Here, the planner should identify five or six such questions or issues to provide examples for and guidance to the speaker as he/she prepares his/her talk.]

- ***Handouts:*** *As you work on your talk, please give attention to developing handouts. They can include material that illustrates your speech or elaborates on the facts that you present. Attendees like to take this kind of information with them for further reference.*

- ***Compensation arrangements:*** *[They might vary for some speakers, such as academics, but they should be spelled out up front.]*

Forms for Organizing Data

I like to develop forms for sending information to and securing it from speakers. Forms organize the data to make it easier to absorb. It is less likely that speakers will miss facts you want them to know if they use the forms to guide them.

There are additional areas that should be communicated to the speakers at certain intervals before the conference. Send the forms when you need the information or when the speaker should take some action with regard to participation.

1. Biographical information

[I send all speakers the following form, which indicates the kind of background facts that we want. In some cases, speakers will have already printed this data about themselves. For those who have not, this form provides guidelines and a place to record this information. Under each area leave blank space so speakers can fill in the information.]

Biographical Information Sheet

Name:

Title:

Your address:

City, state, and zip:

Company or organization:

History with present organization (titles, dates):

Previous employment (organization, titles, dates):

Affiliations with outside organizations (professional societies, trade associations, civic groups):

Areas of recognition (awards, citations, books, and articles):

2. Visual aids desired

[The following form is sent to speakers shortly before the conference. At that point, speakers will have written their talks and should know whether they will want to use audiovisual equipment.]

Request for Audiovisual Equipment

Please check below whether you would like to have audiovisual equipment. Return this sheet in the self-addressed envelope enclosed. [Incidentally, whenever I have information that I want a speaker to return to me, I enclose a self-addressed, metered envelope. I find I get better responses when an individual can fill out a form, put it into an envelope, and drop it in the outgoing mail right away. The cost is negligible compared to the speed of return.]

___I do not need audiovisual equipment

___I need the following equipment:

___35mm Carousel projector

___with remote control

___3 1/4 × 4 slide projector

___16mm sound projector

___VCR

___Chart pad and easel

___Other _____

Your name: _____

Title of your talk: _____

3. **How and when to make hotel reservations**

[This information should be sent early. You want your speakers to be able to get into the headquarters hotel, if they wish, or any other hotel they prefer. If there is a check-off form, it should be sent with instructions about how to complete the form and where to send it. You should know where your speakers will be housed.]

4. **When speaker plans to arrive and leave**

5. **What handouts, if any, the speaker plans to distribute**

[Ask for copies of the handouts to be sure they are not advertising material. If the speaker would like to send the material in advance, provide a pre-addressed label for shipping the handouts.]

6. **Where to pick up registration materials**

[They also should be told what functions they may attend as your guest—sessions, meals, cocktail parties, and so on. The location of the speakers' room should be indicated; this room, sometimes called a greenroom, is a conveniently located room where speakers can go to get help, check on slides and projection equipment, get typing done, and so on.]

7. **Estimated size of the audience**

[You should have a better idea of session sizes as you get closer to the conference date and registrations are coming in. You should give speakers an estimate of audience size not only as a matter of courtesy, but also so they will know how many handouts to bring if they plan to bring them.]

16 | The Talk and the Paper

Many of the speakers chosen to give talks have not had extensive platform experience. They are more familiar with writing papers for publication in magazines or journals. Speakers need to be informed that there is a distinct difference between committing ideas to paper for the print media and delivering an oral presentation to a living, breathing audience of knowledge seekers.

In order to give individuals an understanding of the need to convert their thinking to an oral medium, I prepared a pamphlet and sent it to all the speakers for a certain conference. The material that follows is the actual text from the brochure. My hope was that it would help speakers to orient themselves to the special role they were to play as oral communicators.

Your Role as Author and Speaker

To be effective, anyone who speaks to an audience must capture and maintain interest as a speaker rather than as an author. The person who delivers a speech by reading a paper seldom meets that challenge.

The criticism most frequently leveled at speakers is the tendency to read papers word-for-word. This usually results in a stiff, monotonous delivery that quickly becomes boring. Audiences want to hear a speaker deliver a speech that will highlight key points of the written paper, and that will offer additional facts, observations, and ideas not fully developed in the paper.

The speaker should think of his/her material as having two distinct uses:

1. The *oral presentation* specifically prepared from the paper for the conference audience as an informal, highlighted version of the speaker's ideas.

2. The *written paper* in the form used for publication in professional journals, magazines, or in the conference proceedings, and also used for review by the papers committee.

The Oral Presentation

The speaker can use several techniques so that he/she faces an audience rather than a text:

1. A condensed version of the original paper can be prepared, consisting of key words and phrases as well as whole sentences.

2. Similarly, a detailed outline of the full paper can be developed, each phrase being a major concept or heading.

3. A related technique is to use 3×5 or 6×9 cards. Each card lists a concept, phrase, sentence, or paragraph lifted from the paper itself. It is a useful precaution to number these cards in sequence.

4. If the speaker can feel comfortable only in reading from the paper as originally written, the typing should be double- or, better yet, triple-spaced. This will make it easier for the speaker to follow the lines and to look occasionally at the audience without losing his/her place. The type should be large.

5. When reading, the speaker will find it helpful to have pauses marked in each sentence, such as:

    In any event / the goal is to break up the phrases / in your presentation / so that there is rhythm / to the talk. / This procedure / reduces the monotony / of a speech given / at one pitch.

This approach contrasts to running on rapidly without changes in pace, tone, or inflection.

6. Rehearse your talk ahead of time in front of one or two people, such as your spouse or colleagues. They should be particularly aware of a common trap into which speakers fall, that is, pausing during or after each sentence. Examples of this include "ums," "ers," "ahs," and the like. These interruptions disturb an audience. Rehearsing helps you become aware of these sounds and learn to eliminate them.

7. Though not crucial to the more important concern of developing a talk with stimulating content, there is another aspect to consider in giving a speech. How can you make your presentation more dramatic and innovative so that an audience's attention can be more firmly fixed on what you have to say? Can you use a role play to illustrate a point? Will a questionnaire on issues you will cover that you will ask attendees to fill out at the start of your talk give them greater insights into what they already know and what they will learn from the speaker? You must first develop your content, though. Then, taking a creative approach to presenting ideas is desirable, but not essential.

The Use of Visuals

Visual aids serve one or all of these purposes:

1. They add drama and thus heighten audience interest.

2. They draw attention to a significant point and so add to the learning impact by combining a "picture" with the spoken word.

3. They simplify the presentation of what otherwise might involve complex or extended narration.

Good visual material can contribute greatly to the quality of a speech. On the other hand, visuals consisting of dense lines of words or voluminous figures can be irritating and can detract from an otherwise good paper. Visual material should be clear, not too detailed, visible, and easily understood or read from all parts of the room. If slides are used, 3 1/4 × 4 1/4 are suitable, although 2 × 2 in a carousel are more common.

Exhibit 16.1

Tips in the use of visuals

DON'T	DO
Reproduce a typewritten form to project on the screen.	Blow up one portion of a form and enlarge it in bold lettering.
Display too many figures or too much information. *(The audience will spend its time reading and deciphering the material instead of listening.)*	Extract key words or phrases and allow white space between each line.
Race through too many slides allowing no time to absorb the content.	Select the most important slides, and pause so the facts can be absorbed.
Draw complicated captions, involved labels, or too many separate curves.	Use simple graphs or bar charts with three or four lines per chart.
Present more than one main idea per slide.	Present facts or ideas in steps with separate slides for each, or give secondary ideas verbally.
Show complicated mechanisms.	Divide into several slides with blowups of each important portion.
Use dark photographs or lettering in dark colors on dark backgrounds.	Consult professional photographer about suitable lighting. Crop photos to concentrate on what is important to your talk.

In Exhibit 16.1 are some basic tips to help you produce better visuals.

The Case for Handouts

Better than slides, in many cases, are duplicated handouts. These can contain the forms, charts, and tables that are too complex for slides. Audiences appreciate such papers. A major caveat in distributing handouts before a talk is that curiosity will prompt members of the audience to race through all such written material instead of listening to the talk. If you have sufficient help, distribute a handout at the time you will discuss it. Often it is best to distribute handouts after the talk.

Be sure to have enough sets of handouts for everyone in the audience. This requires checking with the conference planner in advance for a good estimate of attendance for the session.

The Speaker's Responsibility

The speaker must take responsibility for visual material and handouts. The speaker should plan well in advance and rehearse the talk with its accompanying visuals: slides, overhead projection, flip charts, or handouts. You cannot wing it and be successful. (Who rehearses most thoroughly? The professionals. Should an amateur do less?)

A speaker who uses slides is responsible for preparing and transporting them. Immediately after the session, he/she should pick up the tray of slides from the projectionist.

The Written Paper

Note to the Speaker's Secretary:

The speaker's secretary can render an important service to all concerned if he/she will keep reminding the boss of the approaching date of the conference and the stipulated deadline for completion of the paper. The dates can be determined by referring to correspondence from the sponsoring organization.

The manuscript for the paper should not exceed 3,500 words (about 12 to 14 double-spaced pages). It always should be double- or triple-spaced with one-inch margins. Each page should be numbered in consecutive order, with the number centered at the top of the page.

Style and Order

Here are generally accepted specifications for setting up the paper. (The following suggestions do not imply that all papers will include each of these five components. But, where appropriate, follow the style.)

1. **The cover page**

    • The subject of the paper should be at the top of the page.

    • The author's (or authors') name(s), title(s), company, and business address should appear at the bottom of the page.

2. **The second page**

    • It contains the abstract (75 to 100 words).

    • The abstract gives brief highlights of the paper and a statement of its scope and objectives.

3. **The complete manuscript**

    • Bear in mind that any illustrations can be reduced for reproduction. Captions should appear clearly on each illustration. The illustrations should be consecutively numbered, with the number referenced in the text.

    • Tabular material of more than six or eight lines can be included in the text. If tables are longer, place them at the end of the manuscript, each on a separate page. All tables should be numbered separately and in consecutive order. References in the text should be made to the appropriate table number.

4. **Appendixes and acknowledgments**

5. **And last, the bibliography**

    • Bibliographic references should be listed chronologically and contain the following information:

For magazine articles—Title of article, author's full name, magazine, volume number, year, page numbers.

For books—Title, edition, author's full name, publisher, city, year of publication, page numbers.

Importance of Deadlines

Please look at the speech deadline which is indicated in the cover letter. Make note, now, of the date on which the copies of the paper are due. Many speakers not only enter the date on their calendars, but also put a reminder in their tickler files ten days before. It is very important to meet the deadline because many other administrative details are closely geared to the receipt of this material. It is essential to let us know at once if an adjustment in time is required.

17 | Presentation Techniques

We should experiment more with techniques to present information through our speakers. The challenge calls for creativity and alertness to the variety of methods available. With a little ingenuity, you can go beyond the conventional speech/question approach and add spice to the conference diet.

A change of pace in a program adds desirable drama and increases the program's impact on the audience. It enhances the speaker's message.

There are a few techniques you should consider. They suggest what you can do to design a more dynamic conference program. The following is what you should know about their use and effectiveness.

Teleconferencing

The widespread use of teleconferencing, which is the transmission of televised actions from remote sites into the conference room, has not fulfilled its promise as a significant audiovisual adjunct of conferences. Perhaps it has not prospered as expected because it was oversold as a panacea. It was hailed by its promoters as more exciting and effective than meeting face-to-face. Its assets were overblown and its negatives were never mentioned by suppliers. It is too bad. Television does have a place in conferences, if used judiciously.

Either through the use of satellite or cable, one can transmit a talk onto a large screen by a speaker located anywhere in the world. Typically, you would engage a skilled production crew to arrange the transmission. Experts can help to make a presentation more dynamic by varying camera angles, coaching a speaker, and using a prompting device to help the speaker talk from a script with less stress.

Teleconferencing has distinct advantages:

- It offers a good change of pace in a program.

- You can still achieve two-way communication during a question period.

- You can more easily line up a top-level speaker since you can transmit from anywhere, eliminating the speaker's travel time.

- Teleconferencing can dramatize a speaker's presentation.

Conference planners may be apprehensive about using this tool because of the technical skills and crafts it involves. However, if you turn to one of the firms that specialize in this area, it will take complete responsibility for smooth transmission and reception.

The major advice that I would offer, if you plan to use teleconferencing, is to intersperse it in your program. Do not try to rely on this tool as your principal method of presentation. It can become dull if a series of unprofessional speakers is projected for hours. Also, make sure speakers spend enough time rehearsing so that they feel comfortable with the medium.

Telephone Conference Call

At one conference, a key speaker took ill a few days before the meeting was to begin. He was at home, and his doctor would not let him travel. Through the phone company, a conference call was arranged in advance between his home and the conference room. The call was scheduled at the time he normally would have appeared on the program. To coordinate his presentation, we requested and received in advance a copy of his talk, the slides he planned to use, and the handouts he planned to distribute.

His talk from home was amplified over the hotel's sound system. The projectionist, who had a marked copy of the speech, showed the appropriate slides on the screen as the speaker referred to them. A staff member, prepared in advance, used an electric pointer to identify with a lit arrow the areas on the slides to which the speaker referred. Handouts were distributed at times that were keyed to the speaker's remarks. The question period proceeded in the normal way. Written questions were gathered from the audience, directed to the speaker by the chairperson, and answered over the telephone hook-up by the speaker.

This technique should be considered in other applications. It could be used to secure a hard-to-get speaker who might readily accept your invitation if given a choice of speaking from a remote location. A series of slides of the speaker in different poses—while talking on the telephone—provides additional impact.

TelePrompTer

I do not know why greater use is not made of the TelePrompTer at large conferences. It has been employed for many years by presidents since Eisenhower. Ronald Reagan used it for talks from the White House as well as before the groups he addressed. President Bush uses it for his addresses, and it has performed yeoman's service at political conventions. The latest version of the Tele-PrompTer involves the following arrangement:

- Clear plastic screens are placed at an angle in three locations: in front of the speaker, to the left, and to the right of the lectern.

- The speaker's talk is typed in large letters and placed on a roller.

- An operator, controlling the roller, scrolls the copy up at the speed at which the speaker talks. Five lines of text are visible to the speaker. An arrow points to the line where the speaker is at in the text. Should the speaker pause, the operator stops the scroll. Should the speaker digress from the text, the operator stops the scroll and waits for him/her to return to the prepared script.

- The text is projected onto the three plastic screens from black boxes at floor level. The speaker can read the text on the plastic screens from his/her angle of vision. The audience simply sees clear screens. The speaker, looking at the screens, can read his/her talk while seeming to look into the faces of the audience.

The TelePrompTer allows a speaker to reach an audience with lucidity and effectiveness in a far more relaxing style than can be achieved by reading from a speech typed on paper. It takes relatively little rehearsal time for a speaker to feel comfortable with this aid. The scrolled text can be marked for pauses or emphasis to help dramatize the presentation. An association might employ it for its keynote presenters. For company conferences, it is particularly applicable for executive speeches. The system is portable and sets up quickly.

For an international conference attended by 2,500 persons, I recommended the TelePrompTer to our opening speaker. With two rehearsals, he felt comfortable with the system. He delivered his 45-minute talk with confidence and appropriate emphasis, looking directly at attendees in the audience. They did not know he was making eye contact through the plastic screens. After his presentation, more than 50 people approached him to congratulate him on his talk. Some wondered how he was able to give such a well-organized talk without referring to notes, while others expressed admiration for the finest "extemporaneous" talk they had ever heard.

Closed-Circuit TV

There are some segments of a conference program that lend themselves to a talk, a role play, or a panel that can be presented through closed-circuit TV. The presentations are made from another room in the facility. Two cameras and a control board are placed there to pick up the action. Where I have made use of this medium, I have found these advantages:

- It adds drama to a program.

- It offers a desirable change of pace.

- With a skilled technician at the control board, many different effects can be used: split screen, enlargement of visuals, and switching from one panel member to another.

- Even a talk might be presented in this way. Some speakers may be more relaxed in a setting in which they are essentially alone, away from the pressure of facing an audience. You may find they are, thus, more forceful and effective.

Closed-Circuit Use for Small Group

At one conference of 35 top management executives from one company, we recommended the closed-circuit approach. They agreed to try it. The conference was held to review the results of the previous year's sales and to present the budget and programs for the coming year. To serve as background, here is how this company's previous conferences went. The opening session had always been a panel discussion. The participants were the president and three group vice presidents. The vice president of personnel served as chairperson. The entire morning session consisted of the chair's asking questions of panel members and probing for their answers over a 45-minute period. Then the meeting was opened for questions from the audience. The discussion portion of the program took up the rest of the morning session. The four panelists were seated on chairs in front of the attendees.

In the closed-circuit TV format that was introduced on this occasion, the entire panel was in an adjacent room. The president and three group vice presidents were seated as though in a living room, each with a lounge chair and a side table on which they could place notes, reference material, and refreshments. The action was projected on the monitor in the main conference room. The question format was the same as that used in previous years, with the vice president of personnel directing questions to the panel for 45 minutes, after which the panelists moved to the main meeting room for questions from the audience.

After the conference, I asked the vice president of personnel about the results of the morning session. His comments included these points:

- It was the most productive opening they had ever had.

- The panelists felt more relaxed in this informal environment. They were more forthcoming with complete answers. He said it seemed to him that in previous sessions, even though the executives in the audience reported to these men, the panelists were stiffer and more restrained, and weighed their answers to the degree that they were not as revealing.

- The new format allowed increased joking and bantering among the panelists. It added a refreshing pace to the session.

- The panelists apparently felt freer to challenge, in a friendly way, other panelists' observations and to offer a contrary point of view.

Closed-circuit TV is worth considering for other applications. For instance, a speaker might appear on TV and, immediately after his talk, make a dramatic entrance to answer questions.

Rear-Screen Projection

It is not likely that hotels will have a rear-screen system built into their meeting rooms. A few conference centers may. If you want to use rear-screen projection in a hotel, you will have to arrange to have the setup brought in.

Rear-screen projection, as the name implies, projects images from behind the screen. Slides and movies are typically projected from the front of the screen. There is no difference between rear-screen and front-screen projection in terms of the variety of material that can be projected. The advantages of rear-screen projection include the following:

- No one can throw a shadow on the screen by walking in front of the projected image and cutting off its light.

- The distracting noise of the equipment is masked from the audience.

- It is a dramatic way to present material.

Sales meetings frequently use rear-screen projection with exciting effect. It does require a platform of greater depth and a special screen, but the setup is not complicated. It can be handled by a sophisticated audiovisual supplier or a "show producer" that you engage. A rehearsal is recommended for a speaker inexperienced with rear-screen projection, even though it is an easy technique to use.

More company meetings could use rear-screen projection for presentations. Associations could use the approach for their key sessions.

Large-Screen Projector

These projectors can enlarge an image to monumental size. The equipment is used by fight promoters throughout the country. They project live pictures of championship bouts onto huge screens through these projectors and closed-circuit TV.

The conventional equipment used to project film on front screen does not permit you to blow up images as large as those possible with these large-screen TV projectors. If you have a big audience spread throughout a meeting room, consider using a large-screen projector. It will reduce audience eye strain by making it easier to see the projected images. The equipment can be secured through an audiovisual supplier.

Slides, Films, Cassettes, and Transparencies

These visual aids use standard projection equipment. Speakers and conference planners should be encouraged to use visual aids to supplement oral presentations. The engagement of multiple sense organs—sight and hearing—will help to make information more memorable.

It is critical, however, that the speaker be aware not only of the type of graphic to use—bar chart, graph, or key words—but of the equipment that can best project the information. If a visual is too cluttered, the information might be confusing rather than enlightening. If the copy is too small to read easily, the audience will be lost and resentful. In these cases, it is better to use no visuals at all.

Poster Session

You can also present information through a procedure called a poster session. The approach involves a visual display of forms, procedures, brochures, or any type of printed matter. The material is collected in advance from various organizations. By writing to or calling a number of companies before the conference, you can identify what you would like to have them send you. For a personnel meeting, for instance, it might be such material as pre-employment tests, interview forms, employment questionnaires, and employment orientation brochures.

For one meeting, I wrote to 1,500 people, asking them to send us a specific list of such written pieces, pointing out how we would use them. For the poster display, an area was set aside in the conference facility. We put the material on corkboards or let it lie on a table. In each area, we found a person knowledgeable in the subject of the display and asked him/her to stand in the display area to answer questions from attendees. Attendees could visit this area at assigned times or at the conclusion of the day's sessions. In one case, we asked speakers if they had such written or audiovisual material that tied into their talks. If the speakers said yes, we asked them to donate the material to us to use in the display. At the end of the day's sessions, we asked the speakers to come to the poster area to answer questions about any of the material on display there.

One conference on which I worked was in the field of radio programming. I set up one area in the hotel and draped 8 × 10 booths. The booths were divided by the type of format most typically used by radio stations, e.g., rock, top 40, middle-of-the-road, country and western, and classical music. There were five booths, each devoted to a different format. We selected in advance the stations that we wanted to be represented across the United States. We asked them to supply us with three-minute cassettes highlighting how their disc jockeys introduced records; how the stations used jingles to identify themselves; how they handled news; and how they announced contests, if the stations used them. We made four more copies of cassettes for each booth for a total of five. In each booth, we placed a cassette player that would load for the consecutive playing of the five cassettes. Five earphones were placed in each booth, so that five people at a time could listen to the ways in which stations handle the presentation of a range of typical programming. We persuaded each station to send a representative to be at its booth to answer questions. This "poster" session was one of the highlights of the conference.

Dare to Be Different

The ideas expressed in this chapter are intended to encourage conference planners to consider innovative methods of presenting information at a conference. Dare to be different. Experiment. Be creative. Try additional ways to affect your audience. You will earn the gratitude of many attendees who might otherwise have given up on the conference medium as a learning tool.

18 | The Discussion Period

After the talk, the remaining time allocated to a speaker is devoted to a discussion of the subject. This part of the program should be focused on the interests of the audience. There are two objectives to achieve:

1. To give as many participants as possible the opportunity to have their questions answered.

2. To increase even further the information generated by allowing and encouraging contributions from knowledgeable members of the audience. Ways should always be created to tap the experience and expertise of sophisticated professionals in the audience.

For a discussion period to function smoothly, the chairperson should be skilled (as pointed out in Chapter 14) and thoroughly briefed on the responsibilities of the task.

There can be both written and oral participation from the audience, but the participation must not be left to chance. The process must be planned if the result is to be productive.

The Question Process

There is frequently an awkward gap between the time the speaker concludes a talk and when the questions begin to flow from the audience. If questions are not immediately forthcoming, there are approaches to use to fill the time in useful ways.

The chairperson will *not* encourage questions if he/she asks, "Does anyone have a question?" In effect, the chairperson would be daring the audience to come up with a question after the topic has theoretically already been covered, and, in effect, having to publicly admit to being pretty dumb not to have gotten all the information presented.

How to Fill the Gap

Once attendees ask a few questions, their mental gears switch to the question format and to a psychological frame of mind that stimulates participation. Some of the methods I have used successfully to fill the gap before questions emerge include these:

1. Asking the chairperson to write two or three questions during the course of the speaker's presentation.

2. Asking speakers in advance to bring three or four questions to be directed to themselves during the discussion period. Speakers often cannot go into every aspect of their subjects, and this outlet gives them a chance to elaborate on areas they did not have time to touch upon or cover adequately.

   At one conference, this approach backfired. The speaker handed me 15 questions and said these were the only ones he would answer. When the chairperson asked the first question, the speaker turned to a page in his folder and proceeded to *read* his answer. The second question was asked, and the speaker answered it in the same way—straight from his folder. You can imagine my embarrassment. Not only was the spontaneity of the question period lost, but the credibility of the speaker evaporated as well.

3. Give attendees 3 × 5 cards as they enter the meeting room. In the chairperson's opening comments, he/she suggests that attendees write questions as they think of them during the talk itself. The chairperson explains that the question cards will be gathered a few minutes before the speaker's talk ends.

   To facilitate the gathering process, staff members are secured either from the convention bureau or from within the sponsor's organization. The staff members are given written instructions which are reviewed in a briefing session that covers the following points:

   • They are to move slowly down the aisles, looking over the audience for individuals who hold up question cards. The card-gathering process begins five minutes before the conclusion of a talk (before the session, we ask the speaker how long his/her speech will last).

- Without passing in front of the speaker, the staff members take these questions to the chairperson.

    During the discussion period itself, the staff aides patrol the aisles every two minutes to pick up additional questions.

    You might assume that the movement of the staff will create a disturbance while a speaker is talking. If the aides move slowly, their presence is quickly overlooked and actually serves not only as a reminder to the audience to write questions, but also as a stimulus for them to do so. This also alerts the speaker to move on to his/her conclusion.

The chairperson uses the prepared questions only to keep the session flowing and to fill in the time until questions come from the audience. You may not have to ask any of the prepared questions at all if the audience immediately comes forth. The use of the audience's questions is the first priority, no matter how attached the chairperson becomes to the speaker's or his/her own suggestions.

The Associate Chairperson

You can also select an associate chairperson to handle the question period. Although this individual does not have a speaking role, the use of such a person offers several advantages in helping the session to operate more efficiently. The following functions encompass the work the associate chairperson provides.

1. The written questions are brought to the associate chairperson, who, in turn, will follow this procedure:

    - Combine and rewrite into one question those that are generally the same. In this way, the session is not slowed down by repetition.

    - Eliminate questions that are irrelevant.

140 Chapter 18

- Rewrite questions that are difficult to read so that the chairperson will not stumble trying to decipher them.

- Select questions that are the most penetrating and likely to be of greater interest to the audience.

- Pass the questions on to the chair, one by one, giving him/her an opportunity to read the next question in advance.

With the associate's help in handling the written questions, the chair can concentrate more completely on the speaker's answers. Then, if necessary, the chair can probe further, add a comment when appropriate, and, in general, be sure the speaker fully and directly answers the attendee's question.

Prepare and use whatever design or stratagem will work to prompt written questions. Never let this potentially important part of the program lapse into a period of loose, unplanned disorganization. That would tend to undercut the momentum that every speaker should generate.

Oral Questions from the Floor

The oral format, as a supplement to the written question format, offers a desirable change of pace for your question period. The two requirements are: (1) to make sure everyone in the audience can hear the questions; and (2) to make it easy for as many attendees as possible to participate in the discussion period.

In a group of 150 or fewer people, the chair can invite attendees to stand to ask questions without using a microphone. If a question cannot be heard, the chair can repeat it. For larger groups, I have found that these techniques work best:

- Use a wireless microphone. The staff aides, as they move in the aisles, carry this light, portable mike. When an individual signals a desire to speak, the microphone is passed to that person. The participant does not even have to stand; talking directly into the mike, he/she can be heard clearly throughout the room.

- Use a "shotgun" microphone, also called a directional mike. From the front of the room, the mike is pointed at the individual who wants to speak. That person's voice is amplified so that it can carry clearly.

Limitations of Aisle Mikes. One frequently used approach is to place standing microphones in the aisles. Those who want to speak move from their seats, walk to the nearest mike, and, when recognized by the chair, make their comments. There are inherent limitations to this approach. Most members of the audience, I have found, are reluctant to take the trouble, and few have the "bravado" required to stand exposed in the middle of an aisle while waiting to make a comment. With the standing microphone arrangement, you might have much less oral participation than you would using a less conspicuous method.

Problems to Anticipate. Although the oral format is desirable, the chairperson should be aware of certain dangers. The chair must exercise great tact in dealing with the following problems:

- The person who makes a sales pitch for a product or service.

- The individual who gives a long speech, taking up an inordinate amount of the discussion period.

- The audience member who asks a question that is either off the subject or that must be rephrased and refocused because it contains only a kernel of an idea.

- The attendee who, despite the availability of an amplified system, stands to ask a question that doesn't carry to other parts of the room. (Nine times out of ten, the person who declares, "I don't need a mike," truly needs one.)

The chairperson who is aware of these potential problems should be prepared to handle them judiciously.

Telephoned, Recorded Questions

For one company sales meeting, I introduced a procedure that worked well. In the room in which the administrative staff worked, I set up a telephone tied to a tape recorder. Between sessions or after adjournment, any attendee could use his/her room phone to dial the telephone/tape recorder and ask a question of, or direct a comment to, one of the earlier speakers. The caller would leave his/her name and room number. The administrative staff then typed and delivered these recorded messages to the appropriate speaker. When it was convenient, the speaker would dictate a reply to one of the conference staff, who would then type the reply and deliver it to the questioner's room. If the questions or comments were received at the end of the conference, the reply was mailed to the person asking the question. This arrangement permitted individuals to ask questions or make comments that occurred to them after a session ended. Such questions or comments may have been stimulated by an informal discussion subsequently held with colleagues or by an idea occurring to the questioner upon reflection. Even those attendees who did not use this system expressed pleasure at the company's openness and its willingness to provide an opportunity for its speakers to listen and respond to whatever was on the salespeople's minds.

Regional Company Conferences

Many companies hold localized conferences for prospects, customers, or their own staff. These meetings may be called seminars, clinics, workshops, etc. After the talks, these programs typically also hold a discussion period. It is during this part of the conference that the program may begin to fall apart. The officer presiding over these localized meetings may well be a very competent manager, but that doesn't mean that he/she has the knowledge and skills required to handle and design an effective discussion period. The responsibility rests with the national office to suggest the design of the discussion period and to orient and train the individual who will chair the meeting. These elements are essential if the conference is to achieve maximum results.

What Can Happen

I attended a seminar for sales prospects sponsored by the local office of a national company. It was held in a room in the office of this firm and attended by about 150 persons. The program opened with a video presentation. It was professionally and beautifully produced. Short talks in this 12-minute show were given by the company president and other prominent authorities and political figures. Unfortunately, when the discussion period ensued, the meeting began to lose its momentum. The vice president who chaired the conference did little except to make a few introductory remarks and, at the discussion time, announce that questions would be entertained. There were several problems which made this program less productive for the sales effort of this organization.

1. The vice president did not control this portion of the conference. He did not direct the discussion period with the aptitude and firmness necessary to make the time valuable to the audience.

2. The two individuals from the company who formed a panel to answer questions had these problems to overcome:

   • Their chairs, seated at a table, were on the same floor level as the audience. Thus, those of us in the rear of the room could not see them because our views were blocked by the heads of people in front of us. It was frustrating trying to see who was talking.

   • The lighting in the room was projected from "high-hat" fixtures which cast beams straight down. However, none of these lights were directed to the front of the room where the panelists sat. Consequently, they sat in darkness, which was tiring to look at over a period of time.

   • People in the front of the room were continually asking questions. Those in the back could not hear the questions so the answers had little meaning. At one point, someone asked that the questions be repeated. That was done for a while, but then the pattern reverted, and those in the back heard no more questions.

   • Because of the narrowness of the room, those in the rear were too far from the panelists in the front and felt excluded from the proceedings. Midway through the discussion period, attendees in the rear began to leave. They may have had other appointments, but they probably left because they were frustrated with the discussions.

If an old marketing bromide is still valid—that is, that all business is local—companies would do well to look more closely at how to improve their local conferences. They can much more effectively increase sales at a local level than they do today.

19 | Seating for Success

The arrangement of the dais (the platform for speakers' chairs, pronounced "day-us" or "die-us," with the accent on the first syllable), and the chairs and any tables for the audience, deserves more than the cursory attention usually given to it. When thoughtfully planned, seating arrangements can produce several desirable results. They can:

1. Influence the effectiveness of the conference leadership.

2. Encourage greater audience participation.

3. Contribute to engaging and holding the attention of the audience.

Prepare Charts of Rooms

The conference planner should specify room setups when making arrangements at the meeting facility. Charts showing the positions of furniture, with dimensions of placement, should be prepared and given to the department at the meeting facility with whom you have been making arrangements. Decisions on seating arrangements should not be left for the hotel or meeting facility to determine. For larger conferences, your choices of room arrangements may be narrowed by the dimensions and capacities of a big hotel's meeting room or convention center. Even with choices limited by available space, you should take the responsibility to plan the room setup to make it as functional as possible. If you have an option, select the place that will best serve your program purpose.

Dais and Room Dimensions

The platform on which the speakers sit should be one to three feet high, depending on the audience size and the height of the ceiling. Attendees throughout the room should have a clear view of the speakers. The depth of the platform should be eight to ten feet to make it easier for speakers to move their chairs and to walk comfortably to the lectern. If rear-screen projection is used, the depth of the dais must be increased considerably.

I was at one conference where the platform was so narrow that one of the speakers fell off the dais when he moved his chair back to stand up. Fortunately, though he was embarrassed, and the meeting was interrupted, he was not hurt.

Avoid Narrow Rooms

Avoid long narrow rooms for your sessions. If your room is long and narrow, the audience in the rear will be too far from the speakers. Their distance from the "action" at the front makes it more difficult for them to follow the proceedings or take part in the discussions. The formula I have used to determine whether a room is unsuitably long and narrow is this: the length of the room should never exceed its width by more than 50 percent. Thus, if the room is 50 feet wide, it should have a maximum length of 75 feet. If the room is longer than that, you create a "bowling alley" effect.

Arrangement on the Dais

When several speakers are involved in a session and projection equipment is used, use the dais arrangement shown in Exhibit 19.1.

The lectern microphone should be on a flexible gooseneck so that it can be adjusted for the varying heights of the speakers. Use table mikes at the speakers' table. During the discussion period, the speakers can be comfortably seated to answer questions and make or refer to notes. The chairperson stands at the lectern to control the discussion period and directs questions to the appropriate speaker. This arrangement adds a touch of drama as each introduced speaker marches across the platform to the lectern.

Exhibit 19.1

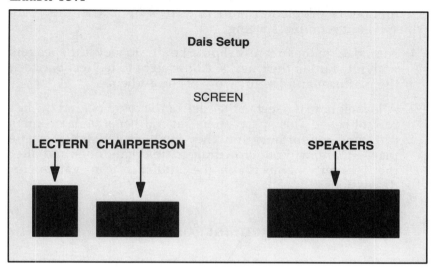

When a screen is on the dais, be sure it is high enough so that the lectern or the speakers do not prevent the projected image from being seen clearly from every part of the room. If the ceiling is too low, place a screen on either side of the dais and use two projectors. If projection is not required, put the lectern in the center of the platform. Wherever the lectern is placed, make sure that when a speaker is looking straight ahead, he/she is viewing a sea of faces rather than an empty aisle.

Audience Seating (with Chairs Only)

1. Place no more than 10 or 12 chairs in a row—from one aisle to the next. This way, there will be less of a problem or disturbance if an individual gets up to leave or another person comes in to take an empty seat.

2. Allow two to two-and-a-half feet between rows. This permits a person to enter or leave a row without forcing others to stand to let him/her pass.

3. Aisles of five to six feet in width are ample, depending on the number of people in the room. Check fire codes: they may spell out required spacing.

4. Attendees in the first row should be able to view the speakers without craning their necks. Allow eight to ten feet between the platform and the first row of the audience.

5. Allow eight to ten feet in the back of the room behind the last row of seats. This space offers several benefits: latecomers can stand comfortably until they can be seated; tables can be placed there, without crowding, to hold handouts; and after the session, members of the audience can gather for discussions.

Arrangement for Tables

If space is available in your meeting room, tables for the audience are desirable, providing individuals with a place to write, and projecting a businesslike appearance. If possible, try to get tables that are one-and-a-half feet wide, or two feet wide at most. If you use the narrower table, you obviously can put more people in a room. Between rows, you need two-and-a-half to three feet. This lets individuals move their chairs back for personal comfort, and still permits others to pass behind those seated without disturbing them. Seat individuals at a table at least two feet apart; two-and-a-half feet provides even more comfort.

For a rough estimate of audience size in a room, with a two-foot table and two-and-a-half feet between individuals, 50 percent fewer persons will be accommodated at tables than can be placed in the same room set with chairs only: 100 people, theater style; 50 people sitting at tables.

Aid to Audience Participation

As I have pointed out previously, one-third to one-half of the time each speaker is scheduled on the program should be set aside for some kind of audience participation. This time not only provides a good change of pace in the program design, it also allows every attendee to personally participate in the conference. It is during this period that a point of uncertainty or misunderstanding can be clarified, a question of application answered, or further information on the subject added.

Audience involvement can be achieved through the way in which you set up the meeting room. One of the arrangements I have used is to set the room in rows of six chairs. At intervals throughout the conference, the chairperson asks attendees in odd-numbered rows to turn their chairs around to face the people sitting in the even-numbered rows. Attendees know whether they are sitting in odd or even rows because row numbers are placed on poles on each side of the auditorium. Or, instead, use alternating colored cards on poles; those in the red rows can be instructed to turn their chairs around and face those in the green rows.

When the groups of 12 are formed (six people facing six), the chairperson can pose a question or issue related to the talk just given. A time limit is set for discussion by each team of 12. The members exchange ideas and conclude with a question to be asked of the speaker. Questions, written on small slips, are collected, and the chairperson poses the questions to the speaker. The audience members return their chairs to their original face-front positions when the speaker begins answering the questions. It sounds complicated, but with clear instructions from the chairperson and alert staff members to help in the first "turnaround," it goes quite well.

Two rows of six persons, 12 in each team, is the upper size limit. Rows of four or five, forming teams of eight or ten, allow for more participation.

Roundtable Discussions

I have also successfully used a roundtable setup to actively involve attendees. Although it was used in conjunction with a certain conference luncheon, the same approach and setup are applicable in any meeting room. Each roundtable of ten people formed the core of a group-involvement project. There were 1,000 people attending this conference. In the morning, three talks were given. The session adjourned at 11:30 a.m., with lunch scheduled for 12:30. The afternoon session was to begin at 2:30.

Before the conference, I selected 200 names from the pre-registration list. I invited these people to serve as chairpersons of lunch table discussions, indicating an 11:30 a.m. meeting where I would outline their responsibilities. A return card was included for their acceptance. A total of 135 people returned their cards, and 110 showed up for the briefing. I reviewed their role as discussion leaders, pointing out that each group was to exchange thoughts on the ideas generated by the morning talks. The discussion of each talk was to last 20–25 minutes. For the final five minutes spent discussing each talk, every group was to develop one or two questions to be asked of the morning speakers.

The luncheon was scheduled to end at 2 p.m. Each chairperson was assigned a table, all of which were numbered.

Before the morning session had adjourned, the chairperson had explained the luncheon procedure to the audience. Attendees were told to sit at any table they liked, but people from the same company were urged to select different tables.

At 2 p.m., the chairpersons took their questions to a pre-designated table where they were deposited into three separate boxes marked with the names of the three speakers. The questions were taken to another room where six volunteers waited. Two individuals had been assigned the questions for each of the three speakers. They read the questions, eliminated duplicates, and selected those that they felt were the most penetrating and of the broadest interest to our audience.

The selected questions were taken to the 2:30 conference room and given to the vice chairperson, who was responsible for organizing the questions and then handing them one by one to the chair, who could then ask the question and concentrate on the answers. This allowed the chair to probe for clear responses. This procedure formed the basis for the entire afternoon discussion.

Conference Room Decor

The conference type that pays the most attention to the "look" of a room is the sales meeting. This type of conference creates visual excitement from the time an attendee enters the meeting until the conference ends.

Since company conferences generally use just one room (association sessions usually are in a multiplicity of rooms), company conference planners should take more notice of the room decor.

One approach to giving life to a room is to engage one of the companies that decorates the exhibits held in the convention centers. These firms have the know-how and the materials on hand to dress up a conference, particularly the principal meeting room. It is refreshing and appealing to walk into a room that is aesthetically attractive, with the dais, speakers' table, and the platform backdrop beautifully draped.

As I have said before, those of us in the conference-planning business are in show business. Give a theatrical flair to your staging. Under all circumstances, if the backdrop of the stage is mirrored or has sconces with lights, cover these distracting elements with some type of drape.

In addition, consider extra lighting to focus on the dais. Often the speakers are in shadows. The dais should stand out from the surrounding area. Some hotels have spotlights in their larger rooms. Use them to draw attention to the speaker. As the speaker is introduced, focus the spotlight on him/her and follow the speaker to the lectern. It adds a touch of drama to the program. Incidentally, a light pink gel over the spotlight adds a healthy glow to a light-skinned speaker who wears no makeup. A stark white light often makes such a speaker look pallid.

20 | How to Rate the Conference Facility

The physical environment—the conference room and its related spaces—has a greater positive or negative impact on a conference than most planners realize. The facility you choose for your conference should be evaluated objectively as part of the planning process. The items that you should consider are in the checklist included in this chapter. A checklist will help you focus on those items that can make a difference in the success of your program. You may use this checklist as a supplement to any list you now use. You can add or subtract items to fit your particular needs. The rating scale suggested allows you to be objective as you evaluate.

As you go through the checklist, select a rating number (including "0") for each item. The number you choose reflects your judgment of how well or how poorly the facility provides the item you are evaluating. Note that the sets of numbers vary from item to item, depending on how important the item is to a conference's success. Thus, an item with ratings running from "0" to "3" is not as important as an item with possible ratings of "0" to "5." Also, some questions under each item will not be as important to you as others. Consider all questions as a group, however.

When you have finished selecting a number for each item, add up your figures. At the end of the chapter you can compare your results with the scale of values provided. With the checklist evaluations, you can determine how good or unsuitable a facility may be for your conference needs. The list also allows you to compare one facility's attributes with another's.

The emphasis in this checklist is on your main conference room. However, the questions can also be adjusted and applied to other rooms you may be using.

Conference Facility Checklist

Rate each of the 17 items. Select and circle a number from those shown for each item, with the **highest number** indicating **"the most suitable"** and **"0"** indicating **"totally inadequate."**

The rating scale is at the end of the chapter. Note that if one of the 17 items is not pertinent, you should not circle a number for that item. The adjustment to your final rating, with this elimination, is explained at the end of this chapter in the section "Facility Rating Scale."

The Main Conference Room

1. Adequacy of lighting   0 1 2 3 4 5

- Is lighting bright enough so that attendees can take notes without straining their eyes? Is it spread evenly throughout the room without high/low shadowing on the walls?

- Do light switches have dimmers so that lights can be lowered for clear projection yet provide enough illumination so that attendees can take notes?

- Are lights placed so that they eliminate fatigue-inducing glare off reflective surfaces?

- Can extra lighting be provided to brighten the dais to make it easier to focus on speakers? (The dais lighting should be brighter than the rest of the room.)

- Are spotlights available to highlight a speaker at the lectern?

2. Quality of sound system   0 1 2 3 4 5

- Can the speaker be heard clearly in all parts of the room without feedback?

- Does the facility provide a variety of microphones, including lavaliere, standing, table, and wireless? Will it provide several of each kind?

- Does the facility provide a control board to adjust the voice levels of various speakers so that adjustments can be made quickly?

3. Proper furniture for desired setup 　　　0 1 2 3 4

- If a classroom setup will be used, is there an adequate number of tables available (preferably of 18-inch or 2-foot widths, to permit more places to be set)?

- When the speaker's platform is set with a screen on it, are the height, width, and depth of the dais sufficient so that the speakers and the projected images on the screen can be clearly seen by all attendees? Is there enough room for speakers to move comfortably?

4. Elimination of distractive decor 　　　0 1 2 3 4

- How well has the facility reduced those features in the room that eventually will tire and divert the participants (loud wallpaper, mirrors, lighted wall sconces, pictures, or windows with distracting views)?

5. Desirable room structure 　　　0 1 2 3 4

- If a screen will be on the speaker's platform, is the ceiling high enough so that attendees can clearly see the projected image and the speakers?

- Is the shape of the room more square than long and narrow? (A long, narrow room will force some unlucky participants to sit in seats that are too far from the front.)

Audience Comfort

6. Proper heating/ventilating/air-conditioning   0 1 2 3 4 5

- Is the system quiet, eliminating air rush noise or rattling sounds from within the system itself?

- Does the system adequately clear the air of odors and smoke?

- Does the heating/ventilating/air-conditioning system provide a comfortable temperature level throughout the room? Can adjustments readily be made?

- Will the system blow air directly on any attendees, making them uncomfortable?

7. Suppression of extraneous sounds   0 1 2 3 4 5

- Can you hear noise from adjacent conference rooms?

- Can you hear noises from such areas as the kitchen, the corridors, or outside?

- Is there carpeting in the conference room to muffle such noises as chairs moving or people walking?

Related Areas

8. Sufficient rooms and locations   0 1 2 3 4

- Does the facility have enough adequately sized conference rooms? (Reserving rooms of various sizes will allow you to place attendees in them without overcrowding or spreading them too thinly in any rooms.)

- Are the rooms close enough to each other so that attendees can find them easily? Are they readily accessible to the conference planner for checking during the conference?

9. Projection booth   0 1

- Is there a separate booth in the conference room for front-screen projection which will mask the noise of the equipment from the audience?

10. Conference rooms 24 hours a day   0 1 2 3

- Can the conference room be set up the night before the program starts so that necessary changes can be made well before the conference begins?

- Can the setup in each room remain each day without being broken down and used for another function?

Free-Time Facilities

11. Recreational/exercise amenities   0 1 2 3 4 5

- Is there a variety of recreational/exercise amenities on site or within easy access and available to attendees (physical fitness area, indoor/outdoor swimming pools, game room, golf, tennis, and jogging path)?

12. Area for informal gatherings   0 1 2 3

- Is there a private area, adjacent to the conference rooms, where participants can go for breaks and socializing away from the noise and crowds of the facility's other guests? Can the area be assigned to this conference only?

Items in the Sleeping Room

13. Work area   0 1 2 3 4 5

- Is a desk available that is large enough for writing and for spreading books and reference materials?

- If two people are assigned to a room, does each get a desk?

- Is lighting over the desk bright enough to allow reading without eyestrain? (Bulbs of 100 watts or more are preferable in areas where work or reading is done.)

- Is there shelving or other suitable space to place workbooks and other conference-related materials?

14. Informal reading   0 1 2 3 4

- Is there a comfortable lounge chair in the room for reading? Is there adequate lighting over the chair to prevent eyestrain?

- Is there a suitably bright light to focus on reading material so the occupant can read in bed?

15. Amenities   0 1 2 3

- How suitable are the amenities in the room for either the male or female business traveler (including shampoo, skin cleanser, cleaning fluid for spots, hair dryer, make-up area with good natural lighting, telephone in bathroom, and outlet to hook up a computer)?

16. Other considerations   0 1 2 3 4 5

- If two are sharing a room, is there a sink outside the bathroom where the second person can wash?

- Is the bathroom large enough to be comfortable?

- How adequate is the security system in the sleeping rooms?

Facility Staff

17. On your initial contact   **0 1 2 3 4 5**

- Were you given sufficient, accurate answers to your questions?

- How difficult was it to get to the person who could give you the information you sought?

- Did the staff ask you the kinds of questions that indicated they understood what could help to make the conference more successful?

- Did the staff offer suggestions that you felt would produce results for your program?

Facility Rating Scale

For each conference you plan, one or more of the 17 items may not be pertinent. In this case, deduct the highest number possible for any item you eliminate from your total score. (Example: If you eliminate item 16, **"Other considerations,"** subtract 5 from each of the rating scales below. In this example, a score of 58–65 would indicate a superior facility; a score of 50–57 would be very good.)

Your Rating Total	Quality of Facility
70 – 63	Superior
62 – 55	Very Good
54 – 50	Satisfactory
49 – 45	Fair
Under 45	Poor

21 | The Facility's Role

This chapter is directed to the places in which conferences are held—hotels, conference centers, resorts, and convention centers. Facilities can make an important contribution to the success of the conference. There are two areas in which their support and insights, if properly used, will make a substantive difference:

- The facility service staff must understand the goals of learning in the conference medium and be able to suggest how the facilities, rooms, and amenities can most contribute to your meeting's success.

- Management should see that meeting rooms and related spaces are specifically designed to enhance the comfort of conference attendees and the effectiveness of the conference leadership.

Management Must Transform its Thinking

If facility management wants to make a difference in these two areas, it must transform its thinking. If change is to occur, it must start at the top management level, not with the staff that services the conference. Above all, management must learn to look at things from a user's point of view if it truly wants to serve the needs of the meetings market. The following changes should be considered:

1. **Reevaluate the design of meeting rooms.** Too often, just plain space is provided, or, in the case of many hotels, rooms that were designed with all the glittering beauty of a ballroom but which are counterproductive for meetings.

Chandeliers, mirrors, wall sconces, and bright, florid wallpaper are not conducive to the effective functioning of a conference. It is understandable that facilities want to maximize the use of their space. However, they must decide whether conferences represent greater profit potential than their social functions do. If so, they must plan rooms for their primary use as meeting space, convertible secondarily for social functions, and not the other way around. Facilities should consider what sort of decor, lighting, audiovisual systems, and furniture will provide the most supportive environment for every aspect of the meeting: conference rooms, sleeping rooms, check-in, conference registration area, signage, area for breaks, and administrative offices.

2. **Appoint one person through whom all client requests are handled.** A constant frustration of conference planners is having to deal with a multiplicity of contacts in a facility. They could range from the front desk, catering, and sales, to convention services, housekeeping, and even the telephone switchboard. The facility should select and train one individual through whom all client information is given and who, in turn, will communicate with all other departments.

3. **Recognize that, for the conference business, a facility is an educational tool.** The goal is learning, and the guestroom is ancillary. All hotels provide clean linen and towels, make beds, and clean rooms. Those services are a given, and most hotels provide them well. If a hotel wants to compete in the meetings business, though, it must expand its field of expertise. It must concentrate on how, through service and amenities, it can help to make a conference more educational and administratively productive.

4. **Develop a more efficient system for providing and securing information at a prospect's initial contact.** In an issue of *Meeting Manager*, a publication of Meeting Planners International, there was an editorial quoting a letter from a member. Its contents represent the feelings of more than a few meeting planners. The letter-writer observed, "I find it astonishing to experience repeatedly, poor, sloppy, underprepared and virtually uncaring sales departments at major

hotels nationwide . . . telephones which are not answered . . . sales departments who disappear, leaving absolutely nobody to check the books when inquiries come in."

Now, lest hotel managers think this complaint is unduly severe and say to themselves, "This can't happen at my hotel," let me suggest an experiment. Call your facility on the telephone and pose as a prospect. Note the response you get. It may be an eye-opener.

I called eight properties throughout the country, saying I wanted to get information for a conference that I might hold in that facility. Here are the results of my calls:

- In all eight cases, I was passed on to two to four persons before finding the right one to handle my inquiry.

- In four cases, when I asked for the rates, the individual gave me the figures, but then immediately added, "But we can negotiate." What a poor sales tactic!

- In another case, I was unable to get the information from the facility I called. I was told to call the headquarters sales office for help. Had I been a prospect, I would have immediately dropped my interest in scheduling a conference in that place.

- In the other three instances, the person to whom I finally talked was cordial. However, in no instance did the person probe with sufficient questions to identify the nature of the conference or my needs and plans, so that he/she could intelligently point out how the facility could uniquely help make my conference a greater success.

If you want to check on an efficient and responsive inquiry system, try calling any of the catalog mail-order houses. Any service business would do well to emulate their approach.

5. **Develop staff capable of offering suggestions to make conferences more successful.** The meeting facility is neither expected nor required to recommend changes in the meeting design or in the program. However, facilities should examine other areas in which they can contribute to the success of a

meeting. Though some facilities may already provide this kind of help, they ought to examine whether these services can be expanded. The type of assistance I refer to is illustrated with these examples:

- **Social and sightseeing activities.** Meaningful contributions can be made by suggesting such social functions as cocktail receptions, dances, theme parties, and interesting places to visit (particularly if a separate program is planned for spouses who attend).

  At one resort/conference center which I co-owned, I appointed an activity coordinator. She developed a series of theme parties, a list of places to visit for sightseeing, and a list of unique off-premises locations for meal functions with unusual menus. When a meeting was booked, she contacted the conference coordinator. In their discussions, they reviewed the creative ideas she developed and considered whether the schedule and the program could include any of the activities. Also brought into the loop and capable of making creative recommendations were the food and beverage director and the executive chef.

- **The setup of the conference rooms.** It would help greatly if there were a staff person in the facility familiar with the advantages and disadvantages, from a learning standpoint, of various room setups: theater arrangement, classroom, roundtable, and horseshoe. That person should be thoroughly familiar with everything about the meeting rooms: their dimensions, kinds and sizes of the furniture on hand or which can be rented, the number of persons that can be realistically seated in each room, and the best setup for the speaker's dais. Then, when the facility staff person talks with the client and learns about the upcoming program, substantive suggestions can be made about the room arrangements that will make the most valuable contribution to the conference.

  Incidentally, facilities should reexamine the printed material they provide listing their meeting rooms and detailing the number of persons the rooms can accommodate in various setups. I have seldom found any relationship between these figures and what I would put into those rooms from the standpoint of participant comfort and the program function. The figures are usually inflated.

6. **Offer help on the administrative work of the meeting.** The typical facility will provide or help to secure any of the equipment a client requests to help do the administrative work of a conference, including typewriters, private office, telephones, and signs. But the facility should go beyond these obvious needs. It should be pro-active. It should conduct research to determine what is generally used and what might be useful to a client in the administration of a program even if it has not been supplied in the past. Could it be personal computers, fax machines, photocopy machines, or portable paging devices? A facility providing these would certainly stand out from the competition. The facility would be opening the client's mind to possibilities perhaps not even considered, and also would be lifting a burden from the shoulders of the coordinator.

7. **Work closely with a client during the course of the conference itself.** One of the gripes that conference planners have with meeting facilities is that the person with whom they have made arrangements—such as the individual mentioned in item 2 of this chapter—is too often not there when the conference actually takes place. In reassessing the role a meeting facility can play in contributing to a conference's results, I would hope that hotels and convention centers might see the necessity of keeping on site—permanently—that valuable person through whom all pre-conference contacts have been channeled. Then, before the opening of the conference, when the client contingent has arrived, a joint facility/client session can be organized. All the key people from any of the hotel departments involved in any phase of the meeting should attend, such as the front desk, food and beverage, convention services, activities director, and housekeeping. Every part of the program should be reviewed in this session, including the responsibilities of each department. If changes must be

made, they could be initiated right there with communication to the right people ensured.

A useful but rarely employed function that conference facilities should consider is one that it can introduce for larger conferences. It involves assigning one of its employees to be with the client's conference coordinator throughout the conference. That person does not have to be a senior staff member. But the employee should be familiar with the operation of the facility and should know all the right personnel to get things done. If a problem arises, this person could be counted on to push the right buttons so that action is taken to get the problem solved *immediately*. What a relief that would be for a client coordinator! From the facility's point of view, it would help ensure a smoothly run program. In addition, this work would provide one of its employees with unusual insights into the mechanism of conferences—a splendid training ground. That knowledge could be quite helpful to a conference facility in the marketing and servicing of conferences in the future—and it would provide a competitive advantage.

I have referred to hotels in many places in this chapter as the places where conferences are held. However, I hope that convention centers recognize that this material is equally applicable to their businesses. These centers are major sites for large conferences. While they do not have sleeping facilities—although many have adjacent commercial hotels—a lot of them do provide food and beverage service for meetings.

Negotiating Rates

Negotiating prices to secure meeting business is a bad practice that besets the hotel industry. This problem is an albatross hanging heavily around the neck of profits. This issue should be studied assiduously by meeting facility managers. They should develop rational policies that can be intelligently and uniformly applied by an informed sales force.

When the price is the principal lever a meeting facility has to offer a client, there is no bottom. There always will be another facility that will offer lower terms. The whole process resembles a bazaar in which the two parties know that the initial quote marks the start of a haggling session. This kind of niggling ritual is good for neither the buyer nor the seller.

To develop policies and procedures that will deal with this all-too-prevalent custom, take these steps. Organize a meeting (which typically will run for several sessions) of all the individuals who come into contact with the conference planners as well as those whose departments will be affected. The meeting agenda should include the following items:

- What benefits do we offer a conference prospect that may be different from and better than the competition's in terms of service, amenities, ambience, conference rooms, and support staff?

- In what ways do these benefits provide advantages to a client that will ease the problems of holding a conference here and help to make that program more productive?

Once you have established the answers to these two questions (and you may want to add others), you have the groundwork to set a range of policies and prices that represent both a good value to prospects and a fair return to you. In setting prices, there are variations that reflect adjustments to factor into these considerations:

1. The number of meeting days (room nights) that the prospect will book. If there is a difference in the actual number of rooms taken, the policy on that difference should be written down and explained up front to the conference planner. Obviously, different discounts should be offered according to the number of rooms booked. But, whatever the variations, they must be uniformly applied and not favor one client over another.

2. The month of the year in which the meeting will be held should be reflected in your pricing schedule.

3. The number of meetings that an organization will guarantee to hold through a year is, of course, another factor to weigh in your pricing decisions.

4. Look also at the kinds and number of social and meal functions you provide and at the income you expect to earn from
   them. Decide how they would affect pricing.

The sales department, which will be implementing the price
strategy, should be thoroughly trained in its application. An informed and believing group of salespeople, who have bought
into the policies because they helped to formulate them, can intelligently explain to a prospect the benefits and advantages of holding a conference in your facility. Clients will respect your rates if
they have a better understanding of the value they will get and
the contribution your facility will make to the success of their
programs.

In the surveys that I have seen concerning what benefits
meeting planners look for in a meeting place, the following are
the ones most frequently cited:

1. Well-designed meeting rooms

2. Courteous and supportive staff

3. Good food

4. Amenities such as indoor swimming pool or health club

5. Pleasant environment

Note that pricing is not mentioned among the users' first five priorities. I don't diminish the importance of price, for it certainly
will play a part in a decision, but it is not the potential client's primary consideration if you can demonstrate how your facility can
uniquely help to produce a more effective meeting.

The Danger of Loose Policies

Here is a dramatic example of the danger of loose pricing policies.
It illustrates the trap of responding to individual pressures to "get
it for less."

One afternoon in my facility, a gentleman approached and
engaged me in a discussion about meetings in general. In the
course of conversation, he related a story that resulted in his moving eight programs to our conference center. He had initially
scheduled them in another facility. He said that one evening at

this other site, he was sitting in the bar talking to another meeting leader who was also holding a program in this place. During the course of their informal discussion, one of them raised the subject of rates. This individual was surprised to learn that the other person, with only two programs a year, was receiving lower rates than he. The following morning, he went to see the general manager to explore the matter. The general manager flew off the handle when the subject was raised. Instead of trying to resolve the problem, he accused this fellow of spying. Shortly thereafter, the man relocated his eight meetings. This is an example of what can happen when rates are set at the whim of the moment (to say nothing of what can happen when the general manager behaves poorly).

Set your rates uniformly, weighing all the factors that have an impact on them. Yielding to the pressures of "getting it for less" will be a significant drag on the profitability and credibility of your facility.

The Challenge for Conference Facilities

This chapter has emphasized the role of meeting facilities as partners in educational conferences. I believe, however, that their approach to serving the conference market has been passive and traditional. Management, I have pointed out, would do well to reexamine those traditional practices. If a facility wants to reach the meetings market, a concentration on selling hotel rooms is misdirected in terms of its marketing and operational strategy. As a user, I will certainly require hotel rooms. But first I want to know what facility managers can do to help my attendees and my conference leadership achieve maximum learning value from our presence in their properties. That challenge and the answers that management provides to this issue can well mean a great difference in profits for the individual facility in the years ahead.

22 | On-Site Operations

A representative of the sponsor's organization usually will visit the conference site before a decision is reached about whether to use the facility. Some planners find it advantageous to make the first visit unannounced. They arrive the night before they plan to make their initial personal contact with the sales department. The aim is to find out early how a typical guest is handled. They use as many services as possible.

The late Mies van der Rohe, the eminent and influential architect, said, "God is in the details." Michelangelo offered a similar thought: "Perfection is made of trifles."

Planning a conference is like producing a play. It is a matter of concept and design—and handling the smallest details. The precision with which a conference functions is related to the degree to which the details of the event are anticipated and executed. Though you will have written and talked with the various support personnel who will be helping you at the conference site, you should set up meetings with them for pre-conference reviews. You want no misunderstandings between you, and no surprises from them.

Meetings Before the Conference Begins

Depending on how complex the program is, I like to go to a facility two or three days before the conference opening. The people at the conference site with whom meetings have been scheduled include the facility staff, the administrative staff, and the staff providing other support services.

The Facility Staff. You will have already sent correspondence spelling out the detailed responsibilities of every department involved with your program and what you need from them. Before coming, you will have arranged the time and place for the meeting with the heads of the departments. The attendees at this session include the general manager and representatives from food and beverage, convention services, sales, front desk, switchboard (telephone operators should know how to handle your calls), engineering, and housekeeping. If there are new people in these functions—different from those with whom you have been in contact—you can learn here who they are.

At this meeting, review the program and the role that each department will play in terms of timing and work during every phase of the conference. Clearly state what you expect in the execution of their responsibilities: smoothness and effectiveness. If facility representatives need any clarification of what you expect, you can discuss it now.

I obtain the extension number of each person present in case I need to make immediate contact. If there is an internal paging system, I obtain that number so that I can reach these individuals. Through the general manager, I try to get someone from the hotel staff assigned to coordinate with me throughout the entire conference. In emergencies, that person, familiar with the hotel operations, knows what to do and whom to call to get immediate action.

The Administrative Staff Whom You Have Engaged to Assist at the Conference. Arrange separate meetings with each of these groups. Distribute written instructions outlining their duties. Review and discuss their responsibilities. The outside personnel that you may need at the conference, if you are not using your own, include the following:

- Individuals in charge of registration.

- Session aides, who will be at the doors of various sessions to handle such work as checking credentials, seating attendees, picking up the written questions, assisting the conference leadership, and working with the projectionist.

- Staff in the headquarters office.

The Other Support Services. The kinds of services that you may require, and will need to contract for separately, include:

- Audiovisual.

- Signs.

- Decorations.

- Sightseeing.

- Spouse program.

- Special events.

- On-site transportation.

At the meetings that have been scheduled with staff providing each of these services, review the instructions you have already given to them. Once again, you will want to be sure that they are thoroughly informed about their responsibilities and how their work can best contribute to the success of your program.

Meetings with Conference Leadership

Meetings with the speakers and the chairpersons of all sessions should be held before the time of their participation. For the morning sessions, hold a breakfast meeting one-and-a-half to two hours before the sessions begin. For afternoon sessions, schedule a luncheon to begin two hours before the afternoon sessions start.

You will have already sent the meeting leadership information about the time and place of these briefing sessions. In the room where you meet, have round tables set up. Place numbers on each table that correspond to the number of each session. In this way, those participating in the same sessions can meet one another and discuss their respective roles.

With the conference leadership—chairpersons and speakers—go over specific functions and instructions.

Chairpersons are to pass on to the attendees at the opening of each session information concerning:

- The hours of the session.

- Location of telephones and restrooms.

- How the question period will be handled (and the sequence of the talks, if there is more than one).

- Availability of printed copies of the talks or cassettes, if any.

- The subject of the session. (Some people will walk into the wrong session by mistake. We want them to go to the session of their choice and not find out halfway through a session that they are in the wrong room.)

- What to do in an emergency.

Speakers are given these facts:

- The setup of the dais and where they will sit.

- How to use the microphone.

- How the question period will be handled.

At this juncture, I ask each speaker the approximate length of his/her talk. This information is useful as a check against the length I have suggested in prior correspondence. It is helpful to the chair and to the session aides who will pick up questions five minutes before the conclusion of each talk. Also, the chairperson has a time commitment in case a speaker goes too far over the announced length. The chair can justifiably slip a note to the speaker suggesting a need to close.

Then:

- A review is made of the audiovisual equipment that has been requested by each speaker. The speakers are told to meet with the projectionist, who will be in the conference room set up to go. They are to explain to the projectionist how they want to coordinate their visuals. Sometimes a speaker brings slides without informing me. We always ask the firm supplying audiovisual equipment to bring extra equipment to cover such emergencies. When this occurs, a staff member is dispatched at once to the audiovisual coordinator. The additional equipment is sent to the meeting room with a projectionist, ready when the speaker arrives.

- Handouts are collected from speakers who have them. We learn when the session aides are to distribute them.

- Room locations are reviewed.

- The latest estimate of attendance in each session is announced.

The objective of these briefing sessions is to ensure that all of the conference leaders are informed about every aspect of their participation. If they are completely informed, they can be more relaxed and comfortable.

The No-Show Problem

On rare occasions, a speaker or a chairperson may not show up for one of many reasons. Before the conference, I will have invited two or three knowledgeable and competent individuals to come to each of the briefing sessions. They may not be needed, but, if they are, they are invaluable. If a chairperson doesn't show, I assign one of the standbys to that session with the back-up material needed to run the session. If a speaker doesn't come, I show the speaker's talk to standbys. Generally, one of the group is familiar with the subject. That standby will read over the speech and deliver it to the audience.

Hold Rehearsals

If a particular conference is a company conference, I suggest that you hold rehearsals at the conference site with all of the executives taking part in the presentation.

Monitor the Sessions

During the conference itself, the conference planner should monitor the sessions continuously. There are seven things to check and correct, if necessary:

1. Are session aides at the doors of the sessions to check credentials and courteously seat latecomers?

2. Can the speakers be heard clearly throughout the room?

3. Is the speaker running overtime?

4. Is the question period running smoothly?

5. How is the coordination with the projectionist going? Does everyone have a clear view of the screen?

6. Is the room temperature comfortable?

7. Are more chairs needed in the room?

In the two to three minutes you spend in each room, you may not be able to check all seven items. However, as you move in and out of the rooms throughout the entire morning or afternoon, you will get a good indication of what is occurring and what corrections are necessary to make those sessions function more effectively for the attendees. The conference planner must be acutely aware that the job is not completed until the last participant leaves for home happy, feeling that the time spent at the conference was eminently worthwhile. So, at the conference itself, the price of success for the conference planner is eternal vigilance.

23 | Organizing the Planning Function

Despite the importance and prevalence of the conference as a medium for learning, few organizations have translated that recognition into a specific professional function or department. It may be because of complacency, satisfaction with present results, or a serious miscalculation of the ease with which conferences are planned. Whatever the reason, organizations are not facing or fully appreciating the following aspects of conference planning:

- The intrinsic purpose of a conference and its inherent potential for audience impact

- The unique skills and wide-ranging insights that a professional conference planner must have, and the significant difference that person can make in the results of a meeting

- The complexity involved in conceiving, developing, and organizing a conference that is stimulating, exciting, memorable, and meaningful in the working life of every attendee

Of the four meeting types cited earlier, only the conference has leadership which is obscured, diffused, or not given sufficient attention or authority. We simply take for granted the kind and amount of leadership required to maximize a program's success. The following analysis highlights the differences among the four kinds of meetings in terms of leadership visibility and purpose:

1. **Discussion meeting.** Leadership requires skills in handling small-group dynamics.

2. **Problem-solving, review, or decision-making meeting.** Its purposes are to discuss programs and changes, resolve issues, and plan future actions. Its leadership qualifications

include knowledge of group dynamics and skill in guiding discussion.

3. **Training and development program.** Its purposes are to communicate knowledge and develop skills in the application of knowledge. Qualifications of leadership include skill in researching the needs and interests of targeted groups and translating these findings into a program that is stimulating and interactive, using a variety of participative and innovative training techniques.

4. **Conference.** Its purpose is to increase attendee knowledge so that wiser decisions can be made and work performed more effectively on the job. Leadership qualifications include professional skill and experience in preparing a conference format such that participant learning is maximized; and understanding of the learning process involved in the conception, development, organization, and execution of this specialized educational activity.

In the discussion and decision-making meetings, it is evident who is in charge, regardless of the chairperson's skills. Similarly, the trainer is clearly running the training program. In the conference, however, too often there is no clear leader with stature and authority to whom everyone else can turn for answers and direction. More frequently, skills and competencies are spread out, resulting in a diffusion of leadership.

Conference Planning as a Profession

It is time that organizations gave the same attention to conference planning as a profession as they did to training and development after World War II. I propose a new "learning machine" that will blend a group of talents into an organizational structure (see Exhibit 23.1, which will be discussed in detail in the next section). Consider the proposed functions representative of the key work to be performed for a conference. You may have different titles to describe these functions. Larger organizations can adapt this structure to a new department staffed by individuals with related skills, while training others with transferable skills. Smaller organizations may have to combine functions or employ a part-time planner and engage outside consultants for other aspects of work. The part-time planner should not throw up his/her hands when faced with the formidable task of planning a professional program. It can be done if the organization has the will to produce a first-class, results-oriented conference, and if top management recognizes the greater value that will come from a professionally planned meeting and supports the work of the appointed part-time planner. Alternatives the part-timer can use to achieve a successful conference include the following:

- Engage outside consultants to do one or more jobs. They are available to perform every phase of conference work quickly and effectively. The part-time planner can coordinate their work.

- Look within your own organization. Are there individuals with skills who can contribute to certain aspects of conference work? Borrow these individuals on a part-time basis.

- Use the free services offered by some travel agents, convention bureaus, hotels, and airlines.

- If a part-time planner can get training in the program planning phase of the conference—the most important part of the process—he/she can use other sources for additional aspects of the conference work.

Organizational Structure

Exhibit 23.1 shows a suggested organizational structure for a full-blown conference planning department. If you are familiar with the job slots that should be filled, you are in a better position to scale down these functions depending on the size of your organization and the frequency with which each type of conference is held. However, even if an organization is small and holds only one conference per year, that meeting should be the best it can be. For the smaller organizations, that goal can be reached with a combination of inside and outside expertise.

Note the positioning of the conference planning department on a level with the training function. Both are necessary to produce a well-rounded employee. The conference provides a forum

Exhibit 23.1

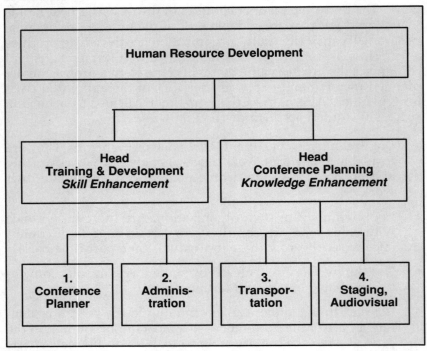

to introduce new techniques or information and to demonstrate how the techniques and information can be profitably applied back on the job. The training program provides "laboratory" experiences that develop skills in the intelligent use of principles, procedures, and programs germane to the work of participants. The four principal elements in conference planning and their positions in the organization follow:

1. **Conference Planner.** This is a new position. Trainers would be good candidates for this position, because they already research, design, and deliver focused training sessions. A conference planner's responsibilities would include such activities as researching information sources, selecting conference topics, creating the meeting design, choosing and

instructing speakers, and overseeing the smooth functioning of the conference program.

2. **Administration.** The planner, employed by many organizations, handles such administrative duties as hotel selection, negotiation, and instruction; staffing the registration operation; arranging for meals and social functions; and handling transportation arrangements, if the organization does not employ a transportation specialist.

3. **Transportation.** A transportation specialist takes care of travel arrangements for the company's personnel. He/she also negotiates with hotels and airlines and other carriers for special rates. Occasionally, the company has a representative from a travel agency on the premises to provide quick service and relieve transportation specialists of some of their work. There is now an association made up of transportation professionals employed in the conference field.

4. **Staging and Audiovisual.** The conference should be viewed as a theater show. As such, the environment of a conference can be exciting and stimulating. Instead of actors, it has speakers. Instead of scripts, it has talks. Instead of a proscenium and sets, it has a dais. Instead of a director, it has a conference planner. The staging function has responsibility for such tasks as "dressing" the room and the dais, for lighting, and for the room setup.

   The audiovisual function already exists in some companies. As part of conference planning, it would handle such assignments as helping speakers to develop visual aids, coordinating the communication technology used, and overseeing the audiovisual aspect of the conference to ensure that it functions effectively.

The Head of Conference Planning

The head of conference planning should possess many special and unusual talents. In addition, he/she must be a manager and a leader. The person who occupies this position should project "stature." For example, if that individual plans a company program, he/she will need diplomacy, knowledge, and a "presence" to guide, direct, and deal with the top executives who will speak at the meeting. The conference planner will need similar attributes to conduct association conferences.

I am not aware of any organization that has, as yet, formalized its conference planning operation into a structure such as that outlined. I hope that, in time, some companies and associations will have the understanding, the vision, and the courage to try setting up a conference planning section. I believe that, if they do test a separate function with variations that suit their environment, they will reduce the waste of time and resources at these meetings and increase the enthusiasm and value experienced by their attendees.

24 | Conference Evaluation

It cannot be stressed enough: it is the needs, problems, and interests of the audience for whom the conference is planned that should be the focus of the conference's design and execution. When the conference is over, the effectiveness of your planning should be measured against the degree to which the program has proven valuable to attendees and the time spent has been worthwhile for them. Such areas as the following should be evaluated:

1. How much knowledge did participants acquire that is better than and different from what they knew before?

2. How useful was the information presented in its practical application to the lives and to the organization of the attendees?

3. How well did the planning and scheduling of the program permit the achievement of maximum benefit from every learning opportunity of the conference, reducing the unproductive time that attendees spent at the conference?

4. How smoothly did the program run, provide efficient help to attendees when needed, and give them a sense of ease and comfort from their participation?

In essence, what you want to determine is how much information was absorbed, how stimulating the process was, and how the productivity and competence of every person was enhanced.

Evaluation Essential for Improvement

The evaluation phase of a conference is essential if the conference is to be strengthened from year to year. We should never be complacent or take a perfunctory, less-than-revealing approach to this analysis. It may turn up uncomplimentary observations that disturb the sponsor, but those observations can be important guidelines to improving the next conference. To be most effective in discerning true attendee reactions, the evaluation process should be objective and anonymous, should reach extensive sources, and should seek detailed answers.

There are two evaluation methods commonly used by many organizations. They are as follows:

1. **Evaluation card at each session.** A card is distributed to attendees as they enter a session. At the opening of the session and at its conclusion, the chairperson asks the participants to check off their rating of the session and the speakers and to turn in the cards at the door as they leave.

2. **Staff queries during conference.** The chair of the meeting, the sponsor, or the conference staff will—throughout the conference—ask a random group of attendees a question such as, "How is the conference going?"

Neither of these techniques nor variations of them are reliable barometers of how effective attendees find a conference. My reservations about the two techniques are these:

- The evaluation card with "excellent," "very good," etc., turned in immediately at the end of a session, produces little of value. Attendees usually haven't taken the time to distance themselves, think deeply, and get some perspective. Answers are given hastily and emotionally, and they contain little qualitative dimension. It is a superficial way to determine how valuable a session or speaker has been. Sponsors using this method may feel that they have honestly attempted to give the audience a chance to express their thoughts—a worthy objective—but they are kidding themselves if they believe they will get an accurate gauge of the value that the conference holds for attendees.

    I attended a session with a speaker whom I judged to be a professional presenter. He told jokes and anecdotes with superb delivery and timing. However, the "hard copy," the material that presented new concepts, ideas, and approaches, was simplistic and thin. Yet the evaluation cards that I saw later virtually all said the speaker was "excellent." Indeed, he was entertaining, amusing, and enjoyable, but his speech lacked substance. There is a place for this type of speaker, if used judiciously. But remember, it is strictly to provide entertainment and not to be confused with valued content for back-home use.

Even when you total the ratings from the cards, you merely have a statistical number. What is behind the figures? The answer may have less to do with the talk than with some personal bias that has led to one's rating.

- Questions asked of attendees during a conference usually draw "kind" responses. Those who respond to questions on conference content or value usually do not want to offend the questioner, who may be the sponsor or from the program committee or the organization's staff. In the rush of activities at a conference, attendees have little time or desire to give thoughtful answers. Polite, superficial observations will not provide answers that will help to improve future meetings. In fact, and possibly worse, such responses give sponsors a false sense of just how useful the program will be in the real world of the participants.

- "Not my people," you say about your attendees. "They'll put it right on the line every time. They'll tell it like it is." You can get a particularly false reading at a company conference. When the boss, under whom the meeting is planned, goes around to employees and asks their opinion of the program, it is unlikely that they will respond critically. More likely, the boss will hear, "Well done," or "Great program," regardless of the conference's quality.

Evaluations that Work

Here are some helpful approaches to conference evaluation. They will produce specific information and in-depth answers to aid both in assessing the success of a particular conference and in helping to plan the next one.

Telephone Interviews. Within a week after the conference ends, select a cross-section of 15 to 20 of its attendees. Prepare a list of open-ended questions to ask them, such as these:

- What information did you get from your attendance do you think will have some applications in your organization?

- In what ways could the conference have been even more valuable to you?

- What aspects of the conference did you find of no particular help?

- Did you prepare a report to summarize your impressions of the conference and what you learned from it? If so, would you send us a copy of the report, if we promise to keep it confidential?

The person who calls should be skilled at interviewing, should explain the purpose of the call and its confidentiality, and should probe with additional questions throughout the interview.

Personal Interviews. The objective of face-to-face interviews is the same as that for telephone interviews. Personal interviews, however, are pre-arranged. A highly selective list of 8 to 12 persons is chosen. For some of these interviews, you may be able to arrange, through an interviewee, a gathering of two to four individuals for a group discussion lasting an hour or an hour and a half. The personal interviews can be set up with individuals located within a 50-mile radius of the person conducting the interview. This person-to-person approach permits you to get an individual's full attention and to observe his/her body language as a guide to further probing.

Small-Group Meetings. Before the conference, contact some members of your staff who worked the conference to arrange a meeting which will take place after the conference is over. In addition, as soon after the conference as convenient, set up a meeting of the program committee if there is one and its members are different from the staff personnel.

The questions posed at these meetings can be taken from those used in the telephone and personal interviews. Add other questions related to improving the efficiency of the whole conference process.

Mailed Questionnaires. Within a week after the conference ends, send a questionnaire to a cross-section of attendees. This timing will have given individuals an opportunity to think about their attendance. Vary the number of questionnaires you send, based on total attendance:

- Fewer than 200 persons, use the entire list.

- 201–500, use 50% of the list, or at least 200.

- 501–1,000, mail to 40%, or at least 300.

- More than 1,000, use 25% of the list, or 300—whichever is larger—with a maximum of 500.

A cover letter should accompany the questionnaire to explain how the recipients were selected, how important the answers are, and how each reply will be carefully used to help strengthen subsequent conferences. Ask that replies be mailed by a certain date. Include a self-addressed, metered envelope. The questions should not call for check-off responses. Rather, they should call for written opinions. Sufficient space, therefore, is obviously needed beneath each question for written replies. You can use the same kinds of questions you use in your personal interviews.

When all of these contributions have been evaluated, the conference planner should write a report. The report will summarize and highlight the material gathered from these various sources plus the conference planner's informed comments. It now becomes the document of record to be used as a springboard and research source for future conferences. The work on the next program can and should begin at this point.

25 | Where to Find Help

There is a range of services and expertise on which a conference planner can call for help in planning many elements of a program or any single part of it. Some of these sources can relieve the planner of a variety of tasks involved in the conference process.

Part-time conference planners represent the majority of those responsible for the conception, development, organization, and execution of this type of meeting. They will find the use of outside experts invaluable when the need arises. Now, the part-timer does not have to solely take on the complexities of effective conference planning—a responsibility for which, typically, the individual has had little training. Rather, outside professionals can supplement the work of part-time planners, permitting the planners to concentrate on coordinating all phases of the program and communicating internally on program progress. Coordinating and communicating are responsibilities in which the part-timer is likely to have experience and competence.

Contributions from Outside

Some organizations have full-time meeting planners who handle the many administrative details of a conference, plus other specialized experts, such as travel managers, who can take care of additional areas of the program. Yet, there still are contributions that outside specialists can make to one or more parts of conference planning.

The various kinds of services available to a conference planner area indicated in the listings that follow. Though I have not identified the names of specific individuals or firms, I have indicated the professional or trade association to which these specialists are likely to belong. If you call these associations, you can obtain an up-to-date list of several consultant services on the subject of your specific need.

You will find some overlap among the different categories. The list provides a range of options.

Categories of Conference Services

1. Administrative Work. This category encompasses many of the administrative details of a conference, including hotel selection and communication, pre-conference registration and correspondence, transportation arrangements, audiovisual coordination, and on-site administration. Many who can provide the service in this area have had extensive experience with a single organization, and now offer their professional counsel as consultants.

American Hotel & Motel Association
1201 New York Avenue, N.W., Suite 600
Washington, DC 20005
202 / 289-3100

> A federation of 50 state and regional hotel associations. Some former hotel executives are now consultants familiar with hotels throughout the country and are aware of their capabilities as conference sites.

American Society of Association Executives
1575 I Street, N.W.
Washington, DC 20005
202 / 626-2723

> Professional society of paid executives of national, state, and local associations in every trade and professional field—technical, engineering, business, profit, and non-profit organizations. Many members who have in the past been responsible

for planning conferences for their associations are now available as consultants.

Meeting Professionals International
4455 LBJ Freeway, Suite 1200
Dallas, TX 75244-5903
972 / 702-3060

Meeting planners, meeting consultants, suppliers of goods and services to meeting planners. This organization has done an excellent job of professionalizing the meeting planning function.

Professional Convention Management Association
100 Vestavia Office Park, Suite 220
Birmingham, AL 35216
205 / 823-7262

Convention coordinators in hotels, managers working to increase the effectiveness of meetings, particularly in medicine, education, and engineering.

Society of Corporate Meeting Professionals
1819 Peachtree NE, Suite 620
Atlanta, GA 30309
404 / 355-9932

Company and corporate meeting planners and hotel convention service managers.

Society of Government Meeting Planners
Frankenberger Place
219 East Main Street
Mechanicsburg, PA 17055
717 / 795-7467

Individuals involved in the planning of meetings held by the government, and suppliers of services to these planners.

2. Audiovisual Equipment. It is not necessary to carry any audiovisual equipment to a conference. Specialized audiovisual houses are present in every major city. They not only supply any type of equipment you require, they also have professional personnel to operate the equipment. Certain facilities, such as conference centers, have equipment on hand which is often supplied as part of their services. When you have chosen a facility, check to see how it handles audiovisual needs.

Audio Visual Management Association
Box 227
607 Arbor Avenue
Wheaton, IL
630 / 653-2772

> Professional society of audio-visual department managers in business and industrial firms.

International Communications Industries Association
11242 Waples Mill Rd, Suite 200
Fairfax, VA 22030
703 / 273-7200

> Suppliers, dealers, manufacturers, and producers of audiovisual products and materials.

3. Coaching the Speakers. Many of the executives on the program at a company conference have not had specific training in speech delivery. Consequently, their style and technique are often dull and monotonous. Consultants in this category can provide one-on-one coaching of these individuals. In addition, packaged training programs are available for in-house group training. In either instance, the help here can result not only in improved presentations, but, subsequently, in greater impact on attendees.

National Speakers Association
1500 South Priest Drive

Tempe, AZ 85281
602 / 968-2552

Professionals responsible for corporate oral communications,
communication consultants, and teachers of oral communications, all of whom are seeking to improve speaking performance in the business world.

4. Developing a Talk. The specialists in this category are experts
in eliminating generalities by sharpening the language in a talk
and replacing dull expressions with more dramatic phrases. They
work with a speaker to maintain the essence of the information
the person wants to communicate, doing so in a style comfortable
for the speaker. The written talk produced can of course still be
adjusted, if desired, but specialists develop a framework from
which to work. These experts can also recommend audiovisual
media to supplement the talk.

Association for Business Communication
Robert J. Myers, Exec. Director
Baruch College, CUNY
Dept. of Speech
17 Lexington Avenue
New York, NY 10010
212 / 387-1620

Individuals or organizations involved in writing for business,
including teachers of business communications, consultants,
training directors, correspondence schools, direct mail copywriters, and public relations directors.

International Association of Business Communicators
One Hallidie Plaza, Suite 600
San Francisco, CA 94102
415 / 433-3400

Communication managers, public relations directors, writers,
editors, and audiovisual specialists who use a variety of

media to communicate with internal and external business audiences.

5. "Dressing up" the Conference Room. The groups proficient in this category add color and attractiveness to the conference room setting. The room will not only be pleasing to the eyes of the attendees as they arrive, it will also provide a relaxing environment within which to listen to a series of talks. The contacts made through the associations listed can either handle this decorating work themselves or recommend sources to which you can turn.

Exhibit Designers and Producers Association
5775 Peachtree Dunwoody, Suite 500-G
Atlanta, GA 30342
404 / 303-7310

Firms designing and building displays for exhibits and trade shows.

International Association of Fairs and Expositions
P.O. Box 985
Springfield, MO 65801
417 / 862-5771

Associations of state, district, and county agricultural fairs on an international basis.

Trade Show Exhibitors Association
5501 Backlick Road, Suite 105
Annandale, VA 22151
703 / 941-3725

Managers and executives of shows, exhibits, and expositions; suppliers are associate members.

6. Entertainment. For special events, theme parties, industrial shows, receptions, and meals, there are many appropriate kinds of entertainment to consider that will add a touch of excitement and change of pace to a conference. The range of entertainers include singers, comedians, dancers, bands, and other acts. For example, dinner theater entrepreneurs will present, with professional performers, condensed versions of hit musicals. Check them for shows that are available. Theme parties can be added with costumes, entertainers, and music. Activities such as these, if provided in a proper setting, can bring an off-beat lift to a program.

Entertainment Industries Council
1760 Reston Parkway, Suite 415
Reston, VA 20190
703 / 481-1414

Individuals from both companies and the entertainment industry, including actors, agents, publicists, producers, directors, and writers. This group's stated purpose is to use the power and influence of the entertainment industry to combat and deglamorize substance abuse.

Showmen's League of America
300 W. Randolph Street
Chicago, IL 60606
312 / 332-6236

Society of Stage Directors and Choreographers
1501 Broadway, Suite 1701
New York, NY 10036
212 / 391-1070

Directors and choreographers in the professional theater.

7. Selecting Outside Speakers. There are many excellent speakers who spend most or all of their time giving talks. They add drama and excitement to a program. Often you can choose a topic from their repertoire. In some cases, they will add material geared to your organization. Many can adjust the length of their presentations to an hour or a day. The talk can be humorous, motivational, or can cover serious business topics. Some of the speakers will be well-known and represented by a speakers' bureau, while others will operate independently. Check the list that follows for that information. You will have to pay a fee to these types of speakers. There are also some speakers whom you can invite who do not charge a fee. In the list of associations, there is a range of options from which to select with no fee. Also, from the various associations listed, you can identify speakers who will provide a desirable balance to your program.

Academy of International Business
College of Business Administration
University of Hawaii at Manoa
2404 Maile Way
Honolulu, HI 96822
808 / 956-3665
www. cba.hawaii.edu/aib/events/1997/cladcall.htm

A worldwide group of university professors, writers, executives, and attorneys involved in education in international business.

American Assembly of Collegiate Schools of Business
600 Emerson Road, Suite 300
St. Louis, MO 63141-6762

Individuals from institutions offering accredited programs of instruction in business administration and accounting at the college level.

Association of American Colleges and Universities
1818 R Street, N.W.
Washington, DC 20009
202 / 387-3760
www.aacu-edu.org

> Individuals from colleges and universities involved in developing effective academic programs in the liberal arts.

National Association for Female Executives
P.O. Box 469031
Escondido, CA 92046
212 / 445-6235
800 / 634-6233
www.nafe.com

> Career women in all phases of business.

National Speakers Association
1500 South Priest Drive
Tempe, AZ 85281
602 / 968-0911
www.nsaspeaker.org

> Members of this association are professional speakers, both those represented by speakers' bureaus and those operating independently.

8. Off-shore Conference Administration. The sophistication that exists in the United States in conference administration is not as advanced in some other countries. If a conference is to be held out of the States, it is important to identify sources for assistance. You want to find an individual or firm, with experience in administering meetings in the foreign country, who knows how to handle and effectively take care of all the problems that could be encountered there.

For contacts, consult associations under the following categories:

- Administrative Work (number 1 in this list)

- "Dressing Up" the Conference Room (number 5)

- Sightseeing (number 11)

- Transportation to the Conference Site and Destination Management (number 13)

9. Production and Staging. The firms in this category view a meeting as theater, providing a range of services. They can develop the entire program, work with each speaker on his/her talk, create visual materials, dress up the room, engage outside humorous or motivational speakers, select the facility, and recommend entertainment. They are used most often to produce industrial shows and sales meetings. But there is no reason that their specialized skills cannot be successfully employed for other kinds of meetings. Some of the firms in this category concentrate on incentive and reward programs and handle every phase of them from promotion to organization and administration.

Society of Incentive Travel Executives
21 W. 38th Street, 10th Floor
New York, NY 10018-5584
212 / 575-0910
www.cicc.egnet.net/site.htm

Individuals involved in the administration or sale of incentive travel including corporate users, incentive travel firms, resorts, cruise lines, hotels, airlines, and tourist boards.

For other contacts, consult the associations listed in the following categories:

- Administration Work (number 1 in this list)

- Entertainment (number 6)

10. Researching Subjects for a Conference. Certain research firms are highly skilled at getting opinions and probing for information from people. They approach an assignment with objectivity. Through sophisticated research techniques, they are able to identify the underlying needs, interests, and problems of a target audience. The results of their work go beyond the superficial answers often given by interviewees. They conduct mail questionnaires and telephone and personal interviews. When you are in the initial stage of identifying the subjects for a program, whether for a company or an association conference, they can produce a true picture of what information will be of greatest help to an audience. The opinion research firms can be useful allies.

American Association for Public Opinion Research
P.O. Box 1248
Ann Arbor, MI 48106
734 / 764-1555
www.aapor.org

> Individuals and firms interested in methods and applications of public opinion and social research.

11. Sightseeing. The scheduling of some conferences leaves time for relaxation. One option is to arrange a sightseeing trip to interesting places in the location where the conference is held. Companies or individuals in that locale who specialize in this field can be of great help. They can provide a choice of the best sights to see and coordinate this entire part of the program.

Gray Line Worldwide
2460 W. 26th Avenue
Building C, Suite 300
Denver, CO 80211
303 / 433-9800
www.grayline.com

Independent charter bus companies that operate sightseeing tours and charter bus service.

12. The Spouse Program. If spouses are invited to a conference and a separate program is to be arranged, there are individuals who can take on the entire responsibility of coordinating a stimulating program. The program can, for example, include talks, sightseeing, visits to unusual places, meals, gifts, and hospitality services.

Refer to groups in the following categories for names of people who can handle this work.

- Administrative Work (number 1 in this list)

- Entertainment (number 6)

- Production and staging (number 9)

- Sightseeing (number 11)

13. Transportation to Conference Site and Destination Management. An organization can save money if it centralizes transportation with one carrier or travel agent. Some carriers and travel agents, aware of the importance of the conference market, have set up a trained conference department to work with clients in this specialized area. Generally, the service is provided without charge.

National Air Transportation Association
4226 King Street

Alexandria, VA 22302
703 / 845-9000
www.nata-online.org

> Key management personnel from aviation service companies, such as fixed based operators and on-demand airtaxis.

National Business Travel Association
1650 King Street, Suite 401
Alexandria, VA 22314-2747
703 / 684-0836
www.nbta.org

26 | What It's All About

Since the invention of the wheel, new technology has been the driving force behind advances in society. Today, it is information technology that has become the transforming agent in American industry. The ability to keep abreast of and secure new, relevant information is central to the ability to cope with ever-changing conditions in the work world and, indeed, in life itself. *Learning, education,* and *training* will be the catchwords and a fresh priority in the decade ahead. In every human activity, organizations are concerned about how best to use these developmental processes for their personnel. We see this phenomenon being played out in the boom in programs involved with continuing professional education.

What We Know and What We Should Know

An ever-widening gap, though, has come between what we know and what we should know. It is the black hole that must be filled if we are to function successfully in the tough competitive universe of the 1990s. Mark Twain expressed the problem in this way: "The difficulties we face in making the right decisions and forming sound judgments are not so much caused by drawing on information that we know—but, using that information we think we know—that isn't so." Benjamin Disraeli, prime minister of Great Britain (1874–1880), observed, "To be conscious that you are ignorant of the facts is a first step to acquiring knowledge."

Of all the educational formats, the conference can be the most progressive, effective medium for communicating information *if* we understand its dynamics and exploit its potential.

In this book, I have tried to emphasize the superior nature of a conference as a unique educational tool. Yet we must face the fact that attendees are expressing widespread dissatisfaction with regard to the value of attendance at too many of our conferences today.

Letitia Baldridge, a former White House aide and public relations consultant, expressed the problem this way: "Taking stock of the 'sustenance' offered up for enduring (conferences) proves one thing: we American business people are tough." Lynn Oppenheim, vice president of the Wharton Center for Applied Research, says, "People often leave a meeting not clear enough about how it connects and what is next."

Conferences that are long on hype and hope and short on sparkle and substance are the targets of many business writers and columnists. They lament, along with many conference attendees, the conferences that do not live up to their billing. The barbs are not simply aimed at American targets. Overseas conferences get their share.

Michael Skapinker, writing in the *Financial Times* of London, decries conferences that do not deliver on promises. He suggests the problem: "It is impossible to stay awake" at conferences. Unlike loyal party members in the U.S.S.R., he declares, most of us "are unused to listening to hours of speeches from gray suits containing even grayer men."

Columnist Skapinker claims that speakers' gems are lost because attendees are put to sleep by too many boring sentences that precede them.

Writing in *Industry Week,* Harvey Gittler reports on the proliferation of conferences sponsored by professional, technical, and trade associations as well as private producers of conferences. Following his summary of current conference fees, he advises, "Companies should be asking what they are getting for their money." His observation is sound. Companies can and do conduct conferences internally. But, to avoid waste, they must make a commitment to provide the talent, time, and attention to this vital medium of learning.

In a column in *The New York Times* on the management of information by libraries of the future, Peter H. Lewis makes this forecast: "Information, rather than oil or steel, is likely to become the most precious commercial resource, and the company that can gather, evaluate and synthesize information ahead of its rivals will have a competitive advantage."

Robert L. Dilenschneider, writing in *The New York Times*, cited the changes in exercising power in the 1990s. He is president and chief executive of Hill & Knowlton, Inc., and author of *Power and Influence: Mastering the Art of Persuasion*. Among the five points he covers in the use of power by executives in industry is: "Gather intelligence relentlessly. Power and influence depend on information. Learn how to absorb vast amounts of it in a focused way." He also cautions, "And do not be misled: the most valuable nuggets are not always in specially commissioned studies."

The fundamental question we should ask ourselves in the use of a conference as a tool of education is: Are we completely aware of the primary role of a conference as a special and distinctive process for converting information into constructive knowledge and the necessity to employ a highly skilled expert to produce a professional program with positive learning results? The process involved in planning a first-class conference is complex and intellectually demanding, and calls for a highly creative, research-oriented mind. If progress is to be made in conference planning, a new generation of thought and a different concept of education, through a conference format, are mandatory.

Is the total conference-planning process outlined in this book arduous to execute? Yes, it is! But then, what successful, creative work is not earned through sweat, dedication, and plain hard work? However, to compromise, ignore, or skip over essential steps to achieving the best possible results in our conferences is to perpetuate their mediocrity.

There is so much to learn. Life is a continuous process of acquiring knowledge. The need to keep individuals well-informed makes conferences more relevant than ever. They communicate information that is practical, understandable, and usable, and give attendees the opportunity to interact with others to validate and solidify that information.

Unfortunately, there has been little in-depth research on conferences as a special field of learning. We can draw conclusions from literature and studies in other fields that relate to the conference process. For example, one of the classic books on adult education is *The Meaning of Adult Education*, by Edward C. Linderman. In the book, Linderman distinguishes the unique character and the different methods and techniques necessary to have an impact on the teaching of mature individuals. Then there is the work proceeding in the field of cognitive theory. It deals with the problem of how individuals gain information and how that information is acted upon in one's work environment.

We can examine, too, the work that has been going on for over a decade at the University of Chicago, where researchers are studying the ways in which the mind can be totally absorbed. The occasions in which that phenomenon occurs are called "flow states." The mind, they indicate, is functioning at its peak then. At that point, motivation, concentration, and a feeling of being able to achieve a high degree of learning are facilitated among individuals. The research concludes that those benefits are experienced more significantly if the learning process is conducted in an environment which is particularly appropriate to the needs and nature of the specific meeting. I elaborated on this key observation in my previous book, *The Total Immersion Learning Environment: Its Critical Impact on Meeting Success.*

Summary of Book

From my experience of more than three decades, let me review some of the points an organization should consider as an orientation and framework when it decides to hold a conference. Anyone challenged to plan a program must be aware of and skilled at hundreds of "do's and don'ts" in terms of principles, concepts, logical and sequential steps, and details that are critical to creating a meaningful, results-oriented conference. The planning of a conference is not achieved with one grand stroke. Broad, innovative thinking is essential, but it is that relentless attention to detail which adds a dimension of cohesiveness, making the difference in a well-constructed conference. Consider some of these factors:

- In our conferences, too frequently, our concept of learning has been carried over from the pedagogical model experienced in our schooling. The *teacher* has the entire responsibility for communicating thought. The *student* remains in a submissive role. This approach presumes that the learner has little knowledge of the subject under discussion.

In the context of a conference, however, we deal with a distinctly different kind of audience: people who are mature, experienced, and motivated to participate. They justifiably will resent sitting for hour after hour being "talked at." Active participation in a conference is essential if we are to keep attendees interested and to broaden their learning. Attendees possess a rich repository of knowledge that should be tapped. Some in the audience may be as informed as the speaker.

- A conference brings together individuals with a variety of expectations and concerns. It is the conference planner's job to anticipate the diversity and aims of a program that is meaningful to all. In your identification of subjects and sessions, make sure they clearly outline what areas the conference will cover. Be as specific as you can. Generalities can diffuse expectations. Participants can come to a conference expecting something different from what is presented, resulting in misunderstandings and negative feelings.

- Peter Drucker, internationally respected business management guru, suggests that executives be reeducated every ten years to stay sharp and up-to-date on changing conditions in the world. In many technical disciplines, the time frame is given as four years for a doubling of information. How can any alert organization exist in the coming decades without competent conference direction which uniquely provides current information?

- Select speakers who will spend time developing talks that follow the guidelines you set. Audiences appreciate those who take time to prepare and who speak with sincerity and depth of knowledge.

  Some speakers may be detached from the words they utter and the ideas they communicate because other people have done the writing and even the thinking for them. An article entitled "Speechwriters and Politicians" discussed one of these writers, who spent five years writing more than 100 talks for members of Congress. He said, "I can recall only two or three times when a speaker gave me enough serious input to help shape a speech." How can we know what a person is thinking when his/her words and ideas in a talk are defined by someone else whose skill lies in shaping words? Indeed, the professional writer has a role to play, but only after the speaker has provided the straw with which to make the bricks.

- A conference can achieve other objectives in addition to transferring information through talks. It brings together people with similar interests and concerns. The camaraderie can serve as a powerful force, depending on how you structure the "free" time of attendees and foster informal discussions among them. It is an opportunity to stretch the learning hours of the day, something each person away from the pressure of his/her work might even welcome. In this context, a participant can experience a relaxing change of pace, making it easier to network with others. This process can serve as an additional motivating factor, giving the attendee a sense of pride for having been selected to attend a conference of peers.

- Make sure the speakers and chairpersons have been thoroughly briefed. It is ironic that those who need it least—the professionals in music, entertainment, and theater—spend great amounts of time preparing for a performance, while those less qualified seldom do. If given a detailed set of instructions in advance, speakers generally will respond with a better presentation that provides these advantages: a logical sequence of ideas, examples of good and bad practices, clarification of obscure points in their field of know-how, suggestions for new applications of previous theory and methodology, and updates of the audience's knowledge quotient.

- Carefully select the setting for your conference. Don't be dazzled by the beauty of a facility or its location, but, more important, look carefully at the meeting rooms, support services and staff, the quality of the sleeping rooms, and the willingness of the food and beverage department to help you arrange social affairs and select your menus. There is no facility that is excellent for every type of meeting. Set your criteria early regarding what you want in a conference site that will contribute maximally to your particular needs.

- It is important to recognize that one needs special skills, knowledge, insights, and experience to produce a distinguished conference. This talent is one that requires an orientation and training program that is different from that for any other group-learning activity. Expertise in the meeting's subject area is not necessary and, indeed, may be a handicap. The crucial ingredient is a professional who understands how people can learn best in the conference environment. That is a skill one can learn. But one is unlikely to possess it merely because he/she has been on previous program committees, has attended other conferences, or has been appointed because he/she happened to be available. In fact, it is unfortunate that the leadership of the conference is too often ill-defined, diffused, or not clearly indicated. We must reach for and assign a professional conference planner to the job, someone with high intelligence who is thoroughly steeped in the dynamics of group learning and who knows how to convert the information presented by a speaker into knowledge that is understandable and applicable in the lives of conference attendees.

- To achieve maximum results from our conferences in the years ahead, we must recognize the conference as a powerful learning medium. We need to challenge our ingrained thinking about how to plan a program that will be of greatest value to participants. We have become so used to providing programs that are ritualistically and traditionally conceived that we have developed stereotyped reactions to conference planning. As a result, we often fail to consider bold, radically new ways to effect change and improvement.

   For example, it was reported at a recent convention of the American Booksellers Association that their meetings would no longer be made up of smoke and mirrors, glitz and glitter. Instead, the meetings would concentrate on a quality program and on books.

   Enthusiasm is an important ingredient to engender in any conference. But when we deal only with frenzy and excitement in a conference, executives who have helped to plan such a meeting can get caught up in their own hyper-bole.

- The properly planned conference can prove its value. It is not only a means of enlightenment, development, stimulation, gratification, morale building, and ego enhancement, but, on the bottom line, it is a means of improving the work process itself. There is no more powerful way to reach a number of people simultaneously and to influence and change them for the better. It is time that organizations step back and examine whether they are getting a maximum return when their employees attend a conference.

History has shown that when people gather face-to-face, share knowledge, and expose attitudes in an open and free forum, an understanding of other points of view is not only possible but likely, with dramatic results. Though our emphasis in this book has been on programs held by companies and associations, the advances in conference planning also have application on a much broader sphere. Through a dialogue among different groups with opposing objectives—countries, issue-oriented groups, political factions—those of us who seek to achieve a world of peace will find that the quintessential process called a conference, when creatively planned by a professional, can be a major contributor to that goal.

About the Author

Coleman Lee Finkel is president and an owner of The Coleman Center in New York City. This is a unique meeting facility in which organizations hold a variety of programs for groups of 10 to 150 participants. Finkel spent four years in extensive research to develop the most effective environment for small meetings; the results of his study, analysis, and experimentation have been incorporated in The Coleman Center.

In his ten years with the American Management Association, Finkel was responsible for a wide range of educational programs in the areas of marketing, general management, finance, and manufacturing. He was promoted to Director of Divisions of AMA, responsible for the work of ten division managers. They, in turn, spearheaded hundreds of meetings of every variety.

Finkel has also been president of the Conference Center Development Corporation (CCDC). This firm has been chosen to consult with more organizations throughout the world for the planning and design of internal meeting facilities than any other group in the United States.

Coleman Finkel has received numerous and prestigious awards. He was winner of the Buzz Bartow Award, the highest honor to be bestowed annually by Meeting Planners International. He received the Torch Award from The American Society for Training and Development for his contributions to the training field. He is the only person to receive both the Torch and the Buzz Bartow Awards.

Among the other citations that honor Finkel's work are the Kilmer Oak Award of Rutgers University for his contributions to the work of the Graduate School of Technical and Vocational Studies. The Professional Communications Society of the Institute of Electronic and Electrical Engineers presented Finkel with a citation "for outstanding contributions to the conception, planning, and design of professional meetings and conference centers."

He is considered a dean among the nation's experts on the planning of learning environments. In an article in *Lodging* magazine, published by American Hotel & Motel Association, Finkel was described as "the nation's number one spokesman and most sought after speaker on conference centers in our country." He was recently selected by *Meeting News* magazine in their 15th anniversary issue as one of the outstanding leaders and thinkers in the country who has made a major impact on the meeting profession over the past 15 years.

About ASAE Publications

The American Society of Association Executives in Washington, DC, is an individual membership organization made up of more than 24,000 association executives and suppliers. Its members manage leading trade associations, individual membership societies, and voluntary organizations across the United States and in 44 countries around the globe. It also represents suppliers of products and services to the association community.

This book is one of the hundreds of titles available through the ASAE Bookstore. ASAE publications keep you a step ahead by providing you and your staff with valuable information resources for executive management, finance, human resources, membership, career management, fundraising, and technology.

A complete catalog of titles is available on the ASAE web site at http://www.asaenet.org or call the Member Service Center at 202/371-0940 for the latest printed catalog.